The Complete Vegetarian Cookbook

Mastering Plant-Based Cooking with a 4-Week Meal Plan for Beginners and Food Lovers

Anna Madison

Copyright © 2024 - All rights reserved.

The content contained within this book may not be reproduced, duplicated, or transmitted without direct written permission from the author or the publisher.

Under no circumstances will any blame or legal responsibility be held against the publisher, or author, for any damages, reparation, or monetary loss due to the information contained within this book. Either directly or indirectly.

Legal Notice:

This book is copyright protected. This book is only for personal use. You cannot amend, distribute, sell, use, quote, or paraphrase any part, or the content within this book, without the consent of the author or publisher.

Disclaimer Notice:

Please note the information contained within this document is for educational and entertainment purposes only. All effort has been executed to present accurate, up-to-date, and reliable, complete information. No warranties of any kind are declared or implied. Readers acknowledge that the author is not engaging in the rendering of legal, financial, medical, or professional advice. The content within this book has been derived from various sources. Please consult a licensed professional before attempting any techniques outlined in this book.

By reading this document, the reader agrees that under no circumstances is the author responsible for any losses, direct or indirect, which are incurred as a result of the use of the information contained within this document, including, but not limited to, — errors, omissions, or inaccuracies.

Introduction 1

Understanding Vegetarianism 4

Environmental and Ethical Considerations 5

Transitioning to Vegetarianism 7

Planning Your Vegetarian Diet 9

Breakfast Recipes 12

    Avocado Toast with Heirloom Tomatoes 12

    Mixed Berry and Almond Smoothie 13

    Sun-Dried Tomato and Feta Frittata 14

    Cinnamon Quinoa Breakfast Bowl 15

    Creamy Mushroom and Spinach Omelette 16

    Pear and Walnut Baked Oatmeal 17

    Zesty Lemon-Ricotta Pancakes 18

    Savory Breakfast Sweet Potato Bowls 19

    Toasted Coconut and Chia Seed Parfait 20

    Spinach and Goat Cheese Breakfast Quesadillas 21

    Golden Turmeric and Ginger Oatmeal 22

    Avocado and Egg Breakfast Pizza 23

    Rustic Tomato and Basil Bruschetta 24

    Almond Butter and Banana Stuffed French Toast 25

    Blueberry Lemon Breakfast Bars 26

    Savory Spinach and Cheese Breakfast Muffins 27

    Peachy Keen Breakfast Quinoa 29

    Green Goddess Avocado Smoothie Bowl 30

Lunch Recipes 31

Mediterranean Chickpea Salad 31
Roasted Vegetable and Quinoa Wrap 32
Grilled Portobello Mushroom Burgers 33
Creamy Butternut Squash Soup 34
Zucchini Ribbon and Cherry Tomato Pasta Salad 35
Curried Lentil and Sweet Potato Bowls 36
Eggplant and Chickpea Stew 38
Avocado, Tomato, and Mozzarella Panini 39
Crispy Tofu and Veggie Stir-Fry 40
Quinoa, Black Bean, and Corn Salad 41
Sweet Potato and Kale Hash 42
Caprese Stuffed Avocado 43
Pesto Pasta with Sun-Dried Tomatoes and Pine Nuts 44
Grilled Vegetable and Goat Cheese Sandwich 45
Beetroot and Feta Cheese Salad 46
Spicy Black Bean Soup 47
Asian-Inspired Tofu Noodle Bowl 49
Mediterranean Stuffed Bell Peppers 50
Warm Spinach and Artichoke Tart 51
Classic Tomato Basil Soup 52
Lemon Herb Couscous Salad 53
Smoky Red Pepper and Chickpea Soup 54

Dinner Recipes 56
Roasted Butternut Squash Risotto 56
Stuffed Portobello Mushrooms with Spinach and Goat Cheese 57
Eggplant Parmesan Tower 58
Quinoa Stuffed Bell Peppers 59
Eggplant Parmesan Tower 61
Garden Vegetable Lasagna 62

- Cauliflower Steak with Chimichurri Sauce 63
- Wild Mushroom and Truffle Oil Risotto 64
- Balsamic Glazed Caprese Skewers 65
- Spinach and Ricotta Stuffed Shells 66
- Roasted Vegetable Tart 68
- Creamy Polenta with Roasted Mushrooms 69
- Lemon Garlic Pasta with Broccoli 70
- Zesty Thai Green Curry with Vegetables 71
- Grilled Vegetable and Goat Cheese Panzanella 72
- Smoky Beet Burgers 73
- Butternut Squash and Sage Gnocchi 74
- Walnut and Lentil Bolognese 75
- Chickpea and Spinach Stuffed Portobello Mushrooms 77
- Sweet Potato and Black Bean Tacos 78
- Roasted Red Pepper Pasta 79

Snacks and Sides 81
- Crispy Baked Zucchini Fries 81
- Avocado and Chickpea Salad 82
- Sweet Potato Hummus 83
- Roasted Brussels Sprouts with Balsamic Glaze 84
- Garlic Parmesan Kale Chips 85
- Quinoa Tabouli 86
- Spicy Edamame 87
- Stuffed Mini Bell Peppers 88
- Cucumber and Dill Greek Yogurt Dip 89
- Oven-Roasted Cauliflower Steaks 90
- Parmesan Herb Popcorn 91
- Beetroot and Goat Cheese Crostini 92
- Carrot Fries with Lemon Herb Dip 93

Mushroom and Garlic Bruschetta 94

Cheesy Spinach Pinwheels 95

Sweet and Spicy Roasted Chickpeas 96

Broccoli and Cheddar Stuffed Potato Skins 97

Tomato Basil Mozzarella Salad 98

Grilled Eggplant Rolls with Herbed Ricotta 99

Savory Pumpkin Seed and Rosemary Crackers 100

A 4-Week Meal Plan 102

Conclusion: Embracing Vegetarianism 114

Introduction

In recent years, we've witnessed a delightful shift in dining tables across the globe—a verdant wave of vegetarianism sweeping through, transforming meals into celebrations of nature's bounty. This resurgence isn't merely a trend but a profound movement towards a more conscious, healthful way of living. At the heart of this green revolution are the myriad benefits that a plant-based diet brings to our health, the environment, and the ethical treatment of animals.

The allure of vegetarianism stems from its promise of vitality and longevity, offering a cornucopia of nutrients while warding off the specters of modern diseases. It whispers the secrets of wellness through every leaf, every root, every fruit. But the embrace of vegetarianism extends beyond the personal, touching the very earth we walk upon. It's an act of kindness—a choice that significantly reduces our carbon footprint, conserving water and sparing the land the heavy burdens of livestock farming.

Moreover, it's a stance of compassion, an ethical choice that refuses to turn a blind eye to the plight of animals. In this way, vegetarianism is more than a diet; it's a harmonious way of life, inviting us to live in alignment with our values and the world around us. As we stand at this crossroads, the path to a healthier, kinder, and more sustainable world is clear—and it is lush with the promise of plant-based abundance.

With this book, I invite you into a world where the vegetables are the stars of the show, where the simplicity of a ripe tomato or the earthy depth of a roasted beet can transform a meal into an experience. This isn't just a cookbook; it's a guide to reimagining your relationship with food, a journey towards a lifestyle that celebrates the abundance and diversity of the plant kingdom. My aim is to gently guide you through the lush gardens of vegetarianism, showing you not just the "whys" but the delightful "hows" of embracing this way of eating and living.

We'll explore together how to transition to a vegetarian lifestyle with grace and ease, making sure that you're not only nourished but satisfied. I'll share with you the secrets of meal planning that turn everyday ingredients into extraordinary meals, ensuring that your journey is as delicious as it is nutritious. And, of course, this book will be brimming with recipes—each one a love letter to the flavors, colors, and textures that make vegetables so exciting.

Whether you're taking your first steps into vegetarianism or looking to deepen your plant-based repertoire, this book is designed to inspire, to teach, and to delight. From the first page to the last, it's an invitation to fall in love with the vibrant world of vegetarian cooking, a celebration of the goodness that comes when we choose to eat with intention and joy.

At its core, vegetarianism is a culinary journey, one that embraces the vast array of fruits, vegetables, grains, nuts, and seeds the Earth offers us. It's a way of eating that celebrates life, focusing on the bounty of the plant world while excluding meat in all its forms. But within this broad canvas, there are nuances and variations, each reflecting different dietary choices and philosophies.

- **Lacto-Vegetarianism** paints with the lush hues of dairy, allowing for milk, cheese, yogurt, and butter. It's a style that marries the richness of dairy with the freshness of plant-based ingredients, creating meals that are both satisfying and deeply flavorful.
- **Ovo-Vegetarianism** adds a different texture to the palette, incorporating eggs. This approach offers flexibility and richness, allowing for the lightness of meringues or the comfort of a soft-boiled egg to complement the earthy notes of vegetables and grains.
- **Lacto-Ovo Vegetarianism** combines the warmth of dairy and the versatility of eggs into the diet, providing a wide spectrum of culinary possibilities. It's a harmonious blend that allows for a vast array of dishes, from the simplest salads to the most elaborate cakes.

- **Veganism** is perhaps the purest expression of plant-based eating, excluding all animal products. It's a compassionate choice that seeks to minimize harm, relying solely on plants for nourishment. This form of vegetarianism challenges us to explore the depths of flavor plants can offer, creating dishes that are as nutritious as they are ethical.

Each variation of vegetarianism invites us to explore our culinary landscape with fresh eyes, to discover new tastes and textures. Whether you're drawn to the inclusive bounty of lacto-ovo vegetarianism or the principled simplicity of veganism, there's a richness to be found in these choices—a celebration of food that honors our health, our planet, and the creatures with whom we share it.

Understanding Vegetarianism

Embarking on a vegetarian journey opens the door to a treasure trove of nutritional riches. This way of eating is not just about what we exclude, but more importantly, what we embrace. Vegetarian diets are abundant in life-enhancing nutrients: think of fiber that whispers secrets to a happy gut, antioxidants that dance gracefully through our bodies fighting free radicals, and a symphony of vitamins and minerals that play the sweetest melody for our health. From the heart-loving omega-3s found in flaxseeds and walnuts to the bone-supporting calcium in leafy greens, each meal is an opportunity to nourish ourselves deeply. In these pages, we'll explore how vegetarian diets, rich in whole, unprocessed foods, become a canvas for not just sustenance, but vibrant well-being.

The tapestry of vegetarianism is woven with threads of not only physical but also profound preventive health benefits. Delve into the pages of research, and you'll find that a diet rich in plants is like a gentle, yet powerful shield against the specters of chronic diseases. Heart disease, type 2 diabetes, and certain cancers find themselves less at home in bodies nourished by fruits, vegetables, and grains. It's as if each leaf and every berry carries its own form of wisdom, teaching our bodies the language of health and resilience.

But the benefits of this verdant diet extend beyond the physical, reaching into the realms of mental health. Imagine the brain as a garden — what we feed it can influence how well it blooms. Studies suggest that the nutrients abundant in a vegetarian diet — such as folate, omega-3 fatty acids, and vitamins B6 and B12 — play a symphony that may help reduce the risk of depression, anxiety, and cognitive decline. It's a compelling narrative: that the food we eat can influence not just how well we live, but also how good we feel.

In this journey through the landscapes of vegetarianism, we'll explore how embracing a diet centered around the bounty of the earth can be a pillar not only for a healthy body but a serene and joyful mind.

Environmental and Ethical Considerations

As we gather around our tables, laden with the vibrant produce that marks a vegetarian lifestyle, we do more than just nourish our bodies. We make a choice that whispers kindness to our planet. Adopting a vegetarian diet is akin to treading more lightly on the earth, each meal a step towards reducing our carbon footprint. The cultivation of plants demands far fewer resources — water, land, and energy — compared to the production of meat. It's a gentle reminder that what we put on our plate has profound implications not just for our health, but for the health of our world.

In these pages, we'll unwrap the layers of how a diet rich in vegetables, fruits, grains, and legumes can be a powerful tool in the fight against climate change. It's a testament to how small, daily decisions can ripple outwards, crafting a future where our planet breathes a little easier, and where our dining choices become acts of environmental stewardship. It's a celebration of food that not only tastes good but does good.

In the quiet moments, when we reflect on the essence of our choices, embracing a vegetarian lifestyle emerges not just as a path to personal health, but as a deeply ethical choice. It's a declaration of our compassion and respect for all living beings. Choosing to center our diets around the fruits of the earth rather than the creatures who walk upon it is a powerful stance on animal welfare. It acknowledges the intrinsic value of every life, seeking to minimize harm and embrace a more peaceful coexistence with the animal kingdom.

This book delves into the heart of vegetarianism not only as a dietary choice but as an expression of our deepest values. It's about extending the warmth and care we have for our loved ones to all creatures, recognizing that the way we eat can be a reflection of our commitment to a kinder, more ethical world. Through the vibrant array of plant-based dishes we explore together, we celebrate a choice that nurtures not only our own wellbeing but the dignity and welfare of animals. It's a journey towards eating in harmony with our ethics, where every meal is a step towards a more compassionate world.

The thread of sustainability weaves through the fabric of vegetarianism, stitching together a lifestyle that respects our planet's finite resources while celebrating the abundance it offers. Embracing vegetarian principles extends beyond the plate, influencing a broader spectrum of choices that collectively contribute to a more sustainable way of living. It's about recognizing our role in the global ecosystem and making thoughtful decisions that reduce waste, conserve energy, and promote the health of our planet.

In this narrative, we explore how the principles of vegetarianism can be integrated into various aspects of daily life, from reducing our reliance on single-use plastics to supporting local farmers and seasonal produce. It's about cultivating a garden, however small, to reconnect with the cycle of growth and harvest, and choosing products that align with our values of compassion and sustainability. This holistic approach to living not only minimizes our environmental impact but also strengthens our connection to the earth and its inhabitants.

By adopting a vegetarian lifestyle, we embark on a journey that is not just about enjoying a diversity of delicious, plant-based foods, but also about crafting a life that is in harmony with our ideals of kindness, sustainability, and wellness. It's a testament to the power of individual choices in shaping a future that is healthy, sustainable, and vibrant for generations to come.

Transitioning to Vegetarianism

Embarking on the path to vegetarianism is like opening the door to a garden bursting with flavors, colors, and possibilities. It's a journey that doesn't require leaps, but rather, thoughtful steps that honor where you are and gently guide you to where you'd like to be. Begin by infusing more plants into your meals, letting vegetables, fruits, grains, and legumes take center stage. Start with one vegetarian day a week, like a "Meatless Monday," gradually increasing as you discover the vast array of dishes and ingredients available.

Embrace the adventure in your kitchen by experimenting with vegetarian recipes that appeal to your palate. Replace familiar meats with hearty alternatives like mushrooms, lentils, and beans to maintain the satisfaction of your meals. Explore international cuisines, many of which offer an abundance of vegetarian options that are both delicious and nourishing.

Remember, transitioning to vegetarianism is a personal journey, one that's enriched by curiosity, learning, and a bit of creativity. Gather inspiration from books, blogs, and perhaps a cooking class or two, allowing the joy of discovery to flavor your journey. Above all, be gentle with yourself, allowing your transition to be a reflection of your own pace, preferences, and lifestyle.

Navigating the social and culinary landscapes as a new vegetarian can feel like hosting a dinner party for guests with varied tastes—it requires a dash of finesse, a spoonful of confidence, and a generous helping of preparation. When dining out, research restaurants in advance to ensure there's a hearty selection of vegetarian options that intrigue your palate. Don't hesitate to communicate with your host or chef about your dietary preferences; more often than not, they're eager to accommodate you with a delicious vegetarian dish that could become your next favorite.

Social situations, from family gatherings to dinner parties, offer a unique opportunity to share your journey and perhaps inspire curiosity about vegetarianism. Bring a dish to share that showcases the richness and satisfaction of vegetarian cuisine—something so delightful that even the most skeptical guests will be tempted to try a bite.

As for cravings, they're natural. Listen to your body and explore vegetarian alternatives that satisfy those cravings. Missing the smokiness of bacon? Smoked paprika on crispy tofu might just hit the spot. Craving a burger? There's a whole world of veggie burgers waiting for you, from black bean to quinoa and beyond.

Remember, every meal is a chance to explore and enjoy. With each challenge comes the opportunity to learn, adapt, and discover new favorites, making your vegetarian journey not just sustainable, but truly enjoyable.

Ensuring nutritional balance as you embrace vegetarianism is like curating a beautiful, diverse garden—it requires mindfulness and a bit of knowledge to flourish. A well-balanced vegetarian diet is rich in variety, incorporating a rainbow of vegetables, fruits, whole grains, nuts, seeds, and legumes. These are the building blocks that provide a symphony of nutrients, each playing its unique role in nourishing your body.

Protein, often a point of concern when transitioning to a vegetarian diet, can be abundantly found in beans, lentils, tofu, tempeh, and seitan, as well as in nuts, seeds, and dairy products for those who include them. For iron, turn to leafy greens like spinach and kale, lentils, and fortified cereals, pairing them with vitamin C-rich foods to enhance absorption. Calcium sources include dairy for lacto vegetarians, fortified plant milks, and green leafy vegetables. Whole grains, nuts, and seeds are excellent sources of magnesium and fiber, while fruits and vegetables offer a bounty of vitamins and antioxidants.

Incorporating a variety of foods not only ensures a nutritional balance but also introduces an exciting array of flavors and textures to your meals. Consider consulting with a nutritionist to tailor your diet to your specific needs, ensuring you're getting the full spectrum of nutrients to support your health. Remember, the journey to a balanced vegetarian diet is an ongoing adventure in nourishment, discovery, and delight.

Planning Your Vegetarian Diet

Planning your vegetarian diet is akin to composing a beautiful, harmonious melody, where each note represents an essential nutrient, coming together to create a symphony of wellness. The key players in this melody are proteins, iron, calcium, omega-3 fatty acids, and vitamins such as B12, D, and zinc, each contributing its unique strength to the ensemble.

Embrace a variety of protein sources like legumes, nuts, seeds, and whole grains, ensuring your body sings with vitality. Iron, a pivotal nutrient for keeping your energy high and your blood healthy, can be found in abundance in leafy greens, legumes, and fortified cereals. Harmonize these with vitamin C-rich foods to enhance iron absorption, creating a perfect duet.

Calcium's notes are essential for strong bones and can be found in fortified plant milks, almonds, and leafy greens, playing a crucial role in your diet's composition. Don't forget the importance of B12, often supplemented, to keep your body's nerve and blood cells healthy, ensuring the melody of your health remains beautiful and vibrant. By carefully selecting your ingredients, you can ensure your vegetarian diet is not just a feast for the senses, but a well-orchestrated symphony of nutrients.

Building a Meal Plan:

Creating a balanced weekly meal plan in the vegetarian kitchen is like sketching a beautiful menu for a week-long feast, where each dish is a thoughtful blend of flavors, colors, and nutrients. Here's a step-by-step guide to orchestrating your weekly culinary symphony:

Step 1: Start with Inspiration Begin by gathering inspiration. Flip through vegetarian cookbooks, browse food blogs, or revisit your favorite recipes. Let the seasons guide you, opting for ingredients that are fresh and abundant.

Step 2: Map Out Your Meals Sketch a rough outline of your meals for the week, including breakfast, lunch, dinner, and snacks. Consider your schedule, planning simpler meals for busier days. Aim for variety to ensure you're covering a broad spectrum of nutrients.

Step 3: Balance Your Plate For each meal, envision your plate filled with vibrant colors. Aim for a balance of complex carbohydrates (like whole grains), protein (from beans, lentils, tofu, or nuts), healthy fats (such as avocados or olive oil), and a rainbow of vegetables and fruits to ensure a symphony of nutrients.

Step 4: Make a Shopping List Based on your meal plan, compile a shopping list, categorizing items by produce, dry goods, refrigerated items, and so on. This organization streamlines your shopping experience and ensures no ingredient is left behind.

Step 5: Prep in Advance Consider what components of your meals can be prepared ahead of time. Washing and chopping vegetables, cooking grains, or making a batch of legumes at the start of the week can save time and simplify meal assembly.

Step 6: Enjoy the Process Remember, cooking is an act of love—both for yourself and those you share your meals with. Allow room for creativity and adjustments based on what feels right for you that week. Cooking shouldn't be a chore, but a joyful journey in exploring the abundance of vegetarian cuisine.

By following these steps, you'll craft not just meals, but experiences that nourish, satisfy, and bring joy. Each week becomes an opportunity to celebrate the diversity and delight of plant-based eating, creating a tapestry of tastes that enrich your vegetarian journey.

Breakfast Recipes

Avocado Toast with Heirloom Tomatoes

Ingredients:

- 2 slices of whole-grain bread
- 1 ripe avocado
- 1 heirloom tomato, sliced
- Salt and freshly ground black pepper, to taste
- Red pepper flakes, optional
- 1 tablespoon of olive oil
- Fresh basil leaves, for garnish

Directions:

1. Toast the slices of whole-grain bread to your liking.
2. While the bread is toasting, halve the avocado, remove the pit, and scoop the flesh into a bowl. Mash the avocado with a fork, seasoning with salt and freshly ground black pepper to taste. Add a pinch of red pepper flakes if you like a bit of heat.
3. Spread the mashed avocado evenly over the toasted bread slices.
4. Top each slice with sliced heirloom tomatoes, slightly overlapping for a beautiful presentation.
5. Drizzle with olive oil and add a few basil leaves for a fresh, aromatic finish.
6. Serve immediately, enjoying the creamy avocado with the juicy sweetness of the tomatoes.

Nutritional Values:

- Calories: 300 (per serving)
- Protein: 6g
- Carbohydrates: 34g
- Fat: 17g

- Fiber: 10g

Mixed Berry and Almond Smoothie

Ingredients:

- 1 cup mixed berries (such as strawberries, blueberries, and raspberries), frozen
- 1 banana, sliced and frozen
- ½ cup unsweetened almond milk
- ¼ cup Greek yogurt, plain
- 1 tablespoon almond butter
- 1 tablespoon honey, or to taste
- A handful of spinach leaves (optional for a green boost)
- A few almonds, for garnish

Directions:

1. In a blender, combine the frozen mixed berries, banana, almond milk, Greek yogurt, and almond butter. Add honey to taste.
2. Blend on high until smooth and creamy. If the smoothie is too thick, you can add a little more almond milk to reach your desired consistency.
3. For a nutritional boost, add a handful of spinach leaves to the blender before mixing. This will give your smoothie a vibrant green color and an extra serving of veggies without compromising the taste.
4. Pour the smoothie into a tall glass and garnish with a few almonds on top.
5. Serve immediately, sipping on this nourishing blend that's perfect for a quick and energizing breakfast.

Nutritional Values:

- Calories: 280 (per serving)
- Protein: 8g

- Carbohydrates: 42g
- Fat: 10g
- Fiber: 7g

Sun-Dried Tomato and Feta Frittata

Ingredients:

- 8 large eggs
- 1/2 cup crumbled feta cheese
- 1/4 cup sun-dried tomatoes, chopped
- 1/4 cup fresh spinach, chopped
- 2 tablespoons fresh basil, chopped
- Salt and freshly ground black pepper, to taste
- 1 tablespoon olive oil
- 1 small onion, finely diced

Directions:

1. Preheat your oven to 375°F (190°C).
2. In a large mixing bowl, whisk together eggs, feta cheese, sun-dried tomatoes, spinach, basil, salt, and pepper.
3. Heat olive oil in an oven-safe skillet over medium heat. Sauté the onion until translucent, about 3-4 minutes.
4. Pour the egg mixture into the skillet, stirring gently to combine with the onion. Cook without stirring for about 2 minutes, until the edges start to set.
5. Transfer the skillet to the oven and bake for 12-15 minutes, or until the frittata is set and lightly golden on top.
6. Remove from the oven, let it cool for a few minutes, then slice and serve.

Nutritional Values:

- Calories: 210 (per serving)
- Protein: 14g

- Carbohydrates: 6g
- Fat: 15g
- Fiber: 1g

Cinnamon Quinoa Breakfast Bowl

Ingredients:

- 1 cup quinoa, rinsed
- 2 cups almond milk
- 2 tablespoons maple syrup, plus more for serving
- 1/2 teaspoon ground cinnamon
- 1 apple, cored and chopped
- 1/4 cup raisins
- 1/4 cup chopped walnuts
- A pinch of salt

Directions:

1. In a medium saucepan, combine quinoa, almond milk, maple syrup, cinnamon, and a pinch of salt. Bring to a boil over medium-high heat.
2. Reduce heat to low, cover, and simmer for 15 minutes, or until most of the liquid is absorbed.
3. Remove from heat and let it stand covered for 5 minutes. The quinoa should be fluffy and creamy.
4. Stir in the chopped apple, raisins, and walnuts.
5. Serve in bowls, drizzled with additional maple syrup to taste.

Nutritional Values:

- Calories: 315 (per serving)
- Protein: 8g
- Carbohydrates: 55g
- Fat: 8g
- Fiber: 6g

Creamy Mushroom and Spinach Omelette

Ingredients:

- 3 large eggs
- 1 tablespoon milk
- Salt and freshly ground pepper, to taste
- 2 tablespoons olive oil
- 1 cup sliced mushrooms
- 1 cup fresh spinach
- 1/4 cup shredded Parmesan cheese
- Fresh chives, chopped for garnish

Directions:

1. In a bowl, whisk together the eggs, milk, salt, and pepper until well combined.
2. Heat 1 tablespoon of olive oil in a non-stick skillet over medium heat. Add the mushrooms and sauté until golden brown and tender, about 5 minutes. Add spinach and cook until just wilted. Remove from the skillet and set aside.
3. In the same skillet, add the remaining tablespoon of olive oil. Pour in the egg mixture, tilting the pan to evenly cover the base.
4. As the omelette begins to set, spoon the mushroom and spinach mixture over half of it. Sprinkle with Parmesan cheese.
5. Carefully fold the other half of the omelette over the filling. Cook for another 2 minutes, or until the cheese begins to melt.
6. Slide the omelette onto a plate, garnish with chopped chives, and serve immediately.

Nutritional Values:

- Calories: 320 (per serving)
- Protein: 22g
- Carbohydrates: 6g
- Fat: 24g

- Fiber: 2g

Pear and Walnut Baked Oatmeal

Ingredients:

- 2 cups rolled oats
- 1 teaspoon baking powder
- 1/2 teaspoon ground cinnamon
- 1/4 teaspoon salt
- 1/4 cup maple syrup
- 2 cups almond milk
- 1 egg, lightly beaten
- 1 teaspoon vanilla extract
- 2 pears, cored and sliced
- 1/2 cup walnuts, chopped
- Additional maple syrup for serving

Directions:

1. Preheat your oven to 375°F (190°C). Grease a 9-inch baking dish.
2. In a large bowl, combine the rolled oats, baking powder, cinnamon, and salt.
3. In another bowl, whisk together the maple syrup, almond milk, egg, and vanilla extract. Pour this mixture over the oat mixture, stirring to combine.
4. Fold in half of the sliced pears and half of the walnuts, then pour the mixture into the prepared baking dish. Arrange the remaining pear slices and walnuts on top.
5. Bake for 35-40 minutes, or until the top is golden and the oats are set.
6. Serve warm, drizzled with additional maple syrup if desired.

Nutritional Values:

- Calories: 265 (per serving)
- Protein: 6g
- Carbohydrates: 38g
- Fat: 10g
- Fiber: 5g

Zesty Lemon-Ricotta Pancakes

Ingredients:

- 1 cup all-purpose flour
- 2 tablespoons granulated sugar
- 1 teaspoon baking powder
- 1/2 teaspoon baking soda
- 1/4 teaspoon salt
- 3/4 cup ricotta cheese
- 1 tablespoon lemon zest
- 1/4 cup lemon juice
- 3/4 cup milk
- 1 egg
- 1 teaspoon vanilla extract
- Butter, for the pan
- Powdered sugar and fresh berries, for serving

Directions:

1. In a large bowl, whisk together flour, granulated sugar, baking powder, baking soda, and salt.
2. In a separate bowl, mix ricotta cheese, lemon zest, lemon juice, milk, egg, and vanilla extract until smooth.
3. Fold the wet ingredients into the dry ingredients until just combined; be careful not to overmix.
4. Heat a non-stick skillet over medium heat and melt a small amount of butter.

5. Pour 1/4 cup of batter for each pancake and cook until bubbles form on the surface, then flip and cook until golden brown on both sides.
6. Serve warm, dusted with powdered sugar and topped with fresh berries.

Nutritional Values:

- Calories: 290 (per serving)
- Protein: 11g
- Carbohydrates: 38g
- Fat: 10g
- Fiber: 1g

Savory Breakfast Sweet Potato Bowls

Ingredients:

- 2 medium sweet potatoes, peeled and diced
- 1 tablespoon olive oil
- Salt and pepper, to taste
- 1 cup cooked quinoa
- 1 avocado, sliced
- 1/4 cup black beans, rinsed and drained
- 1/4 cup red bell pepper, diced
- 2 tablespoons red onion, finely chopped
- 1/4 cup fresh cilantro, chopped
- Lime wedges, for serving
- Hot sauce, optional

Directions:

1. Preheat the oven to 425°F (220°C). Toss the diced sweet potatoes with olive oil, salt, and pepper. Spread them out on a baking sheet and roast until tender and golden, about 25 minutes.

2. To assemble the bowls, divide the cooked quinoa among two bowls. Top with roasted sweet potato, avocado slices, black beans, diced red bell pepper, and red onion.
3. Garnish with fresh cilantro and serve with lime wedges on the side. Add a drizzle of hot sauce if desired.

Nutritional Values:

- Calories: 345 (per serving)
- Protein: 9g
- Carbohydrates: 55g
- Fat: 11g
- Fiber: 10g

These breakfast recipes are designed to bring joy and nourishment to your morning, combining flavors and textures in a way that celebrates the beauty and diversity of vegetarian ingredients. Enjoy the freshness and energy these meals bring to the start of your day.

Toasted Coconut and Chia Seed Parfait

Ingredients:

- 1/3 cup chia seeds
- 1 can (14 oz) coconut milk
- 2 tablespoons maple syrup, plus extra for serving
- 1/2 teaspoon vanilla extract
- 1/4 cup toasted coconut flakes
- 1/2 cup mixed berries (strawberries, blueberries, raspberries)
- A few mint leaves, for garnish

Directions:

1. In a mixing bowl, whisk together chia seeds, coconut milk, 2 tablespoons of maple syrup, and vanilla extract until well combined.

2. Cover and refrigerate for at least 4 hours, or overnight, until the mixture has thickened into a pudding-like consistency.
3. When ready to serve, stir the chia pudding to check consistency, adding a little more coconut milk if needed.
4. Spoon half of the chia pudding into two serving glasses. Add a layer of mixed berries, then sprinkle with some toasted coconut flakes.
5. Repeat the layering process with the remaining chia pudding and top with the rest of the berries and coconut flakes.
6. Garnish with mint leaves and drizzle with additional maple syrup, if desired.

Nutritional Values:

- Calories: 350 (per serving)
- Protein: 5g
- Carbohydrates: 28g
- Fat: 25g
- Fiber: 10g

Spinach and Goat Cheese Breakfast Quesadillas

Ingredients:

- 4 large whole wheat tortillas
- 1 cup fresh spinach leaves, chopped
- 1/2 cup crumbled goat cheese
- 1/4 cup sun-dried tomatoes, chopped
- 1/4 cup red onion, thinly sliced
- 2 eggs, beaten
- Salt and pepper, to taste
- 1 tablespoon olive oil

Directions:

1. In a skillet, heat the olive oil over medium heat. Add the beaten eggs, salt, and pepper, scrambling until just set. Remove from heat.
2. Lay out the tortillas and evenly distribute the scrambled eggs, spinach, goat cheese, sun-dried tomatoes, and red onion among them, covering half of each tortilla.
3. Fold the tortillas in half over the filling.
4. Wipe the skillet clean and return it to medium heat. Cook each quesadilla for about 2 minutes on each side, or until the tortillas are crispy and golden and the cheese has melted.
5. Cut each quesadilla into wedges and serve immediately.

Nutritional Values:

- Calories: 320 (per serving)
- Protein: 14g
- Carbohydrates: 36g
- Fat: 14g
- Fiber: 5g

Golden Turmeric and Ginger Oatmeal

Ingredients:

- 1 cup rolled oats
- 2 cups almond milk
- 1 teaspoon turmeric powder
- 1/2 teaspoon ground ginger
- 1/4 teaspoon ground cinnamon
- 1 tablespoon maple syrup, or to taste
- 1 ripe banana, mashed
- 1/4 cup raisins
- A pinch of black pepper (to enhance turmeric absorption)
- Fresh fruit and nuts, for topping

Directions:

1. In a medium saucepan, bring the almond milk to a low simmer. Stir in the turmeric, ginger, cinnamon, and a pinch of black pepper.
2. Add the rolled oats and raisins to the saucepan, stirring well. Cook over medium heat for 5-7 minutes, or until the oats are tender and have absorbed most of the liquid.
3. Remove from heat and stir in the mashed banana and maple syrup, adjusting the sweetness to your taste.
4. Serve warm, garnished with your choice of fresh fruit and nuts for added texture and nutrients.

Nutritional Values:

- Calories: 300 (per serving)
- Protein: 6g
- Carbohydrates: 62g
- Fat: 5g
- Fiber: 8g

Avocado and Egg Breakfast Pizza

Ingredients:

- 1 pre-baked whole wheat pizza crust (about 9 inches in diameter)
- 1 ripe avocado, mashed
- 2 eggs
- 1/2 cup cherry tomatoes, halved
- 1/4 cup red onion, thinly sliced
- 1/4 cup arugula
- Salt and pepper, to taste
- Red pepper flakes, optional
- 1 tablespoon olive oil

Directions:

1. Preheat your oven to 425°F (220°C). Place the pizza crust on a baking sheet.
2. Spread the mashed avocado evenly over the crust as the pizza base.
3. Carefully crack the eggs onto the avocado, spacing them evenly. Scatter the cherry tomatoes and red onion slices around the eggs.
4. Season with salt, pepper, and red pepper flakes, if using.
5. Bake in the preheated oven for about 10-15 minutes, or until the egg whites are set but the yolks remain runny, and the crust is crispy.
6. Remove from the oven and top with fresh arugula. Drizzle with olive oil before serving.

Nutritional Values:

- Calories: 320 (per serving)
- Protein: 12g
- Carbohydrates: 38g
- Fat: 15g
- Fiber: 6g

Rustic Tomato and Basil Bruschetta

Ingredients:

- 4 slices of sourdough bread
- 2 large ripe tomatoes, finely chopped
- 1/4 cup fresh basil leaves, chopped
- 2 cloves of garlic, minced
- 2 tablespoons extra virgin olive oil, plus more for drizzling
- 1 tablespoon balsamic vinegar
- Salt and freshly ground black pepper, to taste
- 1/4 cup shaved Parmesan cheese (optional, for garnish)

Directions:

1. In a mixing bowl, combine the chopped tomatoes, basil, minced garlic, 2 tablespoons of olive oil, balsamic vinegar, salt, and pepper. Stir together and set aside to marinate for about 15 minutes.
2. Toast the sourdough slices until golden and crispy.
3. Generously top each slice of toasted sourdough with the tomato mixture. Drizzle with a little more extra virgin olive oil and sprinkle with freshly ground black pepper.
4. Garnish with shaved Parmesan cheese, if using, and serve immediately.

Nutritional Values:

- Calories: 200 (per serving without Parmesan)
- Protein: 5g
- Carbohydrates: 27g
- Fat: 8g
- Fiber: 2g

Almond Butter and Banana Stuffed French Toast

Ingredients:

- 4 slices of whole-grain bread
- 1 large ripe banana, sliced
- 4 tablespoons almond butter
- 2 eggs
- 1/2 cup milk (any kind)
- 1 teaspoon vanilla extract
- 1/2 teaspoon ground cinnamon
- Maple syrup, for serving
- Fresh berries, for garnish

Directions:

1. Spread almond butter on two slices of bread and top with banana slices. Place the remaining two slices of bread on top to make sandwiches.
2. In a shallow dish, whisk together the eggs, milk, vanilla extract, and cinnamon.
3. Heat a non-stick skillet over medium heat and lightly grease with butter or oil.
4. Dip each sandwich into the egg mixture, ensuring both sides are well-coated.
5. Cook the French toast sandwiches in the skillet for about 3-4 minutes on each side, or until golden brown and cooked through.
6. Serve warm, drizzled with maple syrup and garnished with fresh berries.

Nutritional Values:

- Calories: 345 (per serving)
- Protein: 12g
- Carbohydrates: 45g
- Fat: 15g
- Fiber: 6g

Blueberry Lemon Breakfast Bars

Ingredients:

- 2 cups rolled oats
- 1 cup almond flour
- 1/2 cup maple syrup
- 1/4 cup coconut oil, melted
- 1 teaspoon vanilla extract
- Zest of 1 lemon
- 1 cup fresh blueberries

- 1/2 teaspoon baking powder
- A pinch of salt

Directions:

1. Preheat your oven to 350°F (175°C). Line an 8x8 inch baking dish with parchment paper.
2. In a large bowl, mix together the rolled oats, almond flour, baking powder, and a pinch of salt.
3. Stir in the maple syrup, melted coconut oil, vanilla extract, and lemon zest until the mixture is well combined.
4. Gently fold in the fresh blueberries.
5. Press the mixture firmly into the prepared baking dish, creating an even layer.
6. Bake for 25-30 minutes, or until the edges are golden brown and the center is set.
7. Allow to cool completely in the dish before cutting into bars.

Nutritional Values:

- Calories: 220 (per bar)
- Protein: 4g
- Carbohydrates: 30g
- Fat: 10g
- Fiber: 4g

Savory Spinach and Cheese Breakfast Muffins

Ingredients:

- 2 cups whole wheat flour
- 1 tablespoon baking powder

- 1/2 teaspoon salt
- 1/2 teaspoon black pepper
- 1 cup fresh spinach, chopped
- 1/2 cup feta cheese, crumbled
- 1/4 cup sun-dried tomatoes, chopped
- 1 cup milk (any kind)
- 1/4 cup olive oil
- 2 eggs

Directions:

1. Preheat your oven to 375°F (190°C). Grease or line a muffin tin with paper liners.
2. In a large bowl, whisk together the whole wheat flour, baking powder, salt, and black pepper.
3. Stir in the chopped spinach, crumbled feta cheese, and sun-dried tomatoes.
4. In another bowl, beat the eggs, then mix in the milk and olive oil.
5. Pour the wet ingredients into the dry ingredients, stirring until just combined (do not overmix).
6. Spoon the batter into the prepared muffin tin, filling each cup about 3/4 full.
7. Bake for 20-25 minutes, or until a toothpick inserted into the center of a muffin comes out clean.
8. Let the muffins cool for a few minutes in the tin before transferring them to a wire rack to cool completely.

Nutritional Values:

- Calories: 180 (per muffin)
- Protein: 6g
- Carbohydrates: 20g
- Fat: 9g
- Fiber: 3g

Peachy Keen Breakfast Quinoa

Ingredients:

- 1 cup quinoa, rinsed
- 2 cups water
- 2 ripe peaches, diced
- 1/2 teaspoon cinnamon
- 1/4 teaspoon nutmeg
- 2 tablespoons maple syrup, plus more for serving
- 1/4 cup chopped pecans, toasted
- 1/2 cup almond milk

Directions:

1. In a medium saucepan, combine quinoa and water. Bring to a boil, then reduce heat to low, cover, and simmer for 15 minutes, or until water is absorbed.
2. Remove from heat and let it stand covered for 5 minutes. Fluff the quinoa with a fork.
3. Stir in the diced peaches, cinnamon, nutmeg, and maple syrup.
4. Serve warm, topped with toasted pecans and a drizzle of almond milk and additional maple syrup if desired.

Nutritional Values:

- Calories: 235 (per serving)
- Protein: 6g
- Carbohydrates: 41g
- Fat: 6g
- Fiber: 5g

Green Goddess Avocado Smoothie Bowl

Ingredients:

- 1 ripe avocado
- 1/2 banana, frozen
- 1/2 cup spinach leaves
- 1/2 cup kale leaves, stems removed
- 1 cup unsweetened almond milk
- 1 tablespoon chia seeds
- 2 teaspoons honey or maple syrup
- 1/4 cup granola, for topping
- Fresh berries and sliced banana, for topping

Directions:

1. In a blender, combine the avocado, frozen banana, spinach, kale, almond milk, chia seeds, and honey or maple syrup. Blend until smooth and creamy.
2. Pour the smoothie mixture into a bowl.
3. Top with granola, fresh berries, and additional banana slices.
4. Serve immediately, diving into this green goddess bowl for a refreshing and energizing start to your day.

Nutritional Values:

- Calories: 320 (per bowl without toppings)
- Protein: 7g
- Carbohydrates: 44g
- Fat: 16g
- Fiber: 11

Lunch Recipes

Mediterranean Chickpea Salad

Ingredients:

- 2 cans (15 oz each) chickpeas, rinsed and drained
- 1 large cucumber, diced
- 1 bell pepper, color of choice, diced
- 1/2 red onion, finely chopped
- 1 cup cherry tomatoes, halved
- 1/2 cup Kalamata olives, pitted and halved
- 3/4 cup feta cheese, crumbled
- 1/4 cup fresh parsley, chopped
- **For the Dressing:**
    - 1/4 cup extra virgin olive oil
    - 2 tablespoons red wine vinegar
    - 1 teaspoon dried oregano
    - 1 clove garlic, minced
    - Salt and pepper, to taste

Directions:

1. In a large bowl, combine chickpeas, cucumber, bell pepper, red onion, cherry tomatoes, olives, feta cheese, and parsley.
2. In a small bowl, whisk together the olive oil, red wine vinegar, dried oregano, minced garlic, salt, and pepper to create the dressing.
3. Pour the dressing over the salad and toss gently to ensure all ingredients are well coated.
4. Let the salad sit for at least 10 minutes before serving to allow the flavors to meld.
5. Serve chilled or at room temperature.

Nutritional Values:

- Calories: 315 (per serving)
- Protein: 10g
- Carbohydrates: 35g
- Fat: 16g
- Fiber: 9g

Roasted Vegetable and Quinoa Wrap

Ingredients:

- 1 cup quinoa, cooked according to package instructions
- 2 bell peppers, sliced
- 1 zucchini, sliced
- 1 yellow squash, sliced
- 1 red onion, sliced
- 2 tablespoons olive oil
- Salt and pepper, to taste
- 4 large whole wheat tortillas
- 1/2 cup hummus
- 1 cup baby spinach leaves
- 1 avocado, sliced
- 1/4 cup goat cheese, crumbled

Directions:

1. Preheat your oven to 425°F (220°C). Toss the bell peppers, zucchini, yellow squash, and red onion with olive oil, salt, and pepper. Spread the vegetables on a baking sheet and roast for 20-25 minutes, or until tender and slightly charred.
2. Warm the tortillas in the oven for a few minutes or on a skillet.
3. Spread a layer of hummus on each tortilla, then add a base of baby spinach leaves.
4. Spoon the roasted vegetables onto the center of each tortilla, followed by quinoa, avocado slices, and crumbled goat cheese.

5. Roll up the tortillas tightly, tucking in the sides as you go.
6. Slice each wrap in half and serve immediately, or wrap tightly in foil to enjoy on the go.

Nutritional Values:

- Calories: 410 (per wrap)
- Protein: 14g
- Carbohydrates: 55g
- Fat: 17g
- Fiber: 12g

Grilled Portobello Mushroom Burgers

Ingredients:

- 4 large Portobello mushroom caps, cleaned and stems removed
- 2 tablespoons balsamic vinegar
- 2 tablespoons olive oil
- 1 garlic clove, minced
- Salt and freshly ground pepper, to taste
- 4 whole-grain burger buns
- 1 ripe avocado, sliced
- 1 tomato, sliced
- 1 small red onion, thinly sliced
- 1 cup arugula
- Mayonnaise or vegan aioli, for spreading

Directions:

1. In a small bowl, whisk together balsamic vinegar, olive oil, minced garlic, salt, and pepper. Brush this mixture over both sides of the Portobello mushrooms.

2. Preheat your grill or grill pan over medium heat. Grill the mushrooms for about 5 minutes on each side, or until they are tender and juicy.
3. Toast the burger buns lightly, if desired.
4. To assemble the burgers, spread a little mayonnaise or vegan aioli on the bottom halves of the buns. Place a grilled mushroom on each, followed by avocado slices, tomato slices, red onion, and arugula. Top with the other half of the bun.
5. Serve immediately, enjoying the meaty texture and rich flavors of the Portobello mushroom.

Nutritional Values:

- Calories: 390 (per burger)
- Protein: 9g
- Carbohydrates: 45g
- Fat: 20g
- Fiber: 7g

Creamy Butternut Squash Soup

Ingredients:

- 1 medium butternut squash, peeled, seeded, and cubed
- 1 tablespoon olive oil
- 1 small onion, chopped
- 3 cups vegetable broth
- 1 cup coconut milk
- 1 teaspoon curry powder
- Salt and freshly ground pepper, to taste
- Pumpkin seeds and fresh cilantro, for garnish

Directions:

1. In a large pot, heat the olive oil over medium heat. Add the chopped onion and sauté until translucent.

2. Add the cubed butternut squash and cook for a few minutes, stirring occasionally.
3. Pour in the vegetable broth, bring to a boil, then reduce the heat and simmer until the squash is tender, about 20 minutes.
4. Remove from heat and let it cool slightly. Blend the soup using an immersion blender or in batches in a regular blender until smooth.
5. Return the soup to the pot, stir in the coconut milk and curry powder, and season with salt and pepper. Heat through.
6. Serve the soup in bowls, garnished with pumpkin seeds and fresh cilantro.

Nutritional Values:

- Calories: 220 (per serving)
- Protein: 3g
- Carbohydrates: 30g
- Fat: 11g
- Fiber: 5g

Zucchini Ribbon and Cherry Tomato Pasta Salad

Ingredients:

- 8 oz whole wheat pasta (such as penne or fusilli)
- 2 medium zucchinis
- 1 cup cherry tomatoes, halved
- 1/2 cup Kalamata olives, pitted and sliced
- 1/4 cup pine nuts, toasted
- 1/2 cup fresh basil leaves, torn
- 1/4 cup extra virgin olive oil
- 2 tablespoons lemon juice
- 1 clove garlic, minced

- Salt and freshly ground black pepper, to taste
- 1/4 cup grated Parmesan cheese (optional)

Directions:

1. Cook the pasta according to package instructions until al dente. Rinse under cold water and drain.
2. Using a vegetable peeler or mandoline, slice the zucchinis into thin ribbons.
3. In a large bowl, combine the cooked pasta, zucchini ribbons, cherry tomatoes, olives, pine nuts, and basil.
4. In a small bowl, whisk together the olive oil, lemon juice, minced garlic, salt, and pepper to create the dressing.
5. Pour the dressing over the pasta salad and toss gently to combine.
6. Serve chilled or at room temperature, garnished with grated Parmesan cheese, if using.

Nutritional Values:

- Calories: 320 (per serving)
- Protein: 9g
- Carbohydrates: 45g
- Fat: 12g
- Fiber: 6g

Curried Lentil and Sweet Potato Bowls

Ingredients:

- 1 cup dried green lentils, rinsed
- 1 large sweet potato, peeled and cubed
- 1 tablespoon olive oil
- 1 teaspoon curry powder
- 1/2 teaspoon ground turmeric
- 1/2 teaspoon ground cumin

- 4 cups baby spinach leaves
- 1/4 cup coconut milk
- Salt and freshly ground black pepper, to taste
- Fresh cilantro, for garnish
- Cooked brown rice or quinoa, for serving

Directions:

1. In a medium saucepan, bring 2 cups of water to a boil. Add the lentils, reduce heat to low, cover, and simmer for 20-25 minutes, or until tender.
2. Meanwhile, toss the cubed sweet potato with olive oil, curry powder, turmeric, and cumin. Roast in a preheated 425°F (220°C) oven for 20 minutes, or until tender and caramelized.
3. In the last few minutes of cooking, stir the coconut milk into the lentils and season with salt and pepper. Add the spinach to the lentils, cover, and cook until the spinach has wilted.
4. To serve, spoon the lentil mixture over a bed of cooked brown rice or quinoa. Top with roasted sweet potato, and garnish with fresh cilantro.

Nutritional Values:

- Calories: 370 (per serving without rice/quinoa)
- Protein: 18g
- Carbohydrates: 58g
- Fat: 9g
- Fiber: 15g

Eggplant and Chickpea Stew

Ingredients:

- 2 tablespoons olive oil
- 1 large eggplant, cubed
- 1 onion, diced
- 2 cloves garlic, minced
- 1 can (15 oz) chickpeas, drained and rinsed
- 1 can (14.5 oz) diced tomatoes, undrained
- 1 teaspoon ground cumin
- 1/2 teaspoon smoked paprika
- 1/2 teaspoon ground coriander
- Salt and freshly ground black pepper, to taste
- 2 cups vegetable broth
- Fresh cilantro, for garnish
- Cooked couscous, for serving

Directions:

1. Heat the olive oil in a large pot over medium heat. Add the cubed eggplant and cook until it starts to soften, about 5 minutes.
2. Add the diced onion and minced garlic, cooking until the onion is translucent.
3. Stir in the chickpeas, diced tomatoes with their juice, cumin, smoked paprika, coriander, salt, and pepper. Mix well to combine.
4. Pour in the vegetable broth and bring the stew to a simmer. Reduce the heat to low and continue to cook, covered, for 20 minutes, or until the eggplant is tender and the flavors have melded.
5. Serve the stew over cooked couscous, garnished with fresh cilantro.

Nutritional Values:

- Calories: 280 (per serving, without couscous)
- Protein: 9g
- Carbohydrates: 45g
- Fat: 8g
- Fiber: 13g

Avocado, Tomato, and Mozzarella Panini

Ingredients:

- 4 large slices of sourdough bread
- 1 avocado, sliced
- 1 tomato, sliced
- 4 ounces fresh mozzarella cheese, sliced
- Fresh basil leaves
- Salt and freshly ground black pepper, to taste
- 2 tablespoons olive oil or softened butter, for grilling

Directions:

1. Assemble the panini by layering slices of avocado, tomato, and mozzarella cheese between two slices of bread. Add fresh basil leaves and season with salt and pepper.
2. Brush the outside of each sandwich with olive oil or softened butter.
3. Heat a panini press or a grill pan over medium heat. Place the sandwiches in the press or on the grill pan, pressing down lightly. If using a grill pan, you may need to flip the sandwich to grill both sides evenly.
4. Grill until the bread is golden and crispy and the cheese has melted, about 3-5 minutes.
5. Slice each panini in half and serve hot.

Nutritional Values:

- Calories: 400 (per sandwich)
- Protein: 15g
- Carbohydrates: 45g
- Fat: 20g
- Fiber: 6g

Crispy Tofu and Veggie Stir-Fry

Ingredients:

- 14 oz firm tofu, pressed and cubed
- 2 tablespoons cornstarch
- 3 tablespoons olive oil, divided
- 2 cups broccoli florets
- 1 red bell pepper, sliced
- 1 carrot, sliced thinly
- 2 garlic cloves, minced
- 1 tablespoon ginger, minced
- 1/4 cup soy sauce
- 2 tablespoons maple syrup
- 1 tablespoon rice vinegar
- 1 teaspoon sesame oil
- Salt and pepper, to taste
- Cooked rice or noodles, for serving
- Sesame seeds and sliced green onions, for garnish

Directions:

1. Toss the cubed tofu with cornstarch until well coated.
2. Heat 2 tablespoons of olive oil in a large pan over medium-high heat. Add the tofu and fry until crispy on all sides. Remove from the pan and set aside.
3. In the same pan, add the remaining olive oil, broccoli, bell pepper, and carrot. Stir-fry until the vegetables are just tender.

4. Add the garlic and ginger, cooking for another minute until fragrant.
5. In a small bowl, whisk together the soy sauce, maple syrup, rice vinegar, and sesame oil. Pour over the vegetables in the pan, adding back the crispy tofu. Stir everything to combine and heat through. Season with salt and pepper, to taste.
6. Serve hot over cooked rice or noodles, garnished with sesame seeds and green onions.

Nutritional Values:

- Calories: 350 (per serving, without rice)
- Protein: 18g
- Carbohydrates: 30g
- Fat: 20g
- Fiber: 4g

Quinoa, Black Bean, and Corn Salad

Ingredients:

- 1 cup quinoa, rinsed
- 2 cups vegetable broth
- 1 can (15 oz) black beans, drained and rinsed
- 1 cup corn kernels (fresh, canned, or thawed from frozen)
- 1 red bell pepper, diced
- 1/4 cup fresh cilantro, chopped
- 1 avocado, diced
- Juice of 2 limes
- 2 tablespoons olive oil
- 1 teaspoon ground cumin
- Salt and pepper, to taste

Directions:

1. In a medium saucepan, bring the vegetable broth to a boil. Add the quinoa, reduce heat to low, cover, and simmer for 15 minutes, or until all the liquid is absorbed. Remove from heat and let it stand for 5 minutes, then fluff with a fork.
2. In a large bowl, combine the cooked quinoa, black beans, corn, red bell pepper, cilantro, and avocado.
3. In a small bowl, whisk together the lime juice, olive oil, cumin, salt, and pepper. Pour over the quinoa salad and toss to combine.
4. Refrigerate for at least 30 minutes before serving to allow the flavors to meld.

Nutritional Values:

- Calories: 290 (per serving)
- Protein: 10g
- Carbohydrates: 45g
- Fat: 8g
- Fiber: 10g

Sweet Potato and Kale Hash

Ingredients:

- 2 large sweet potatoes, peeled and diced
- 1 tablespoon olive oil
- 1/2 teaspoon smoked paprika
- Salt and freshly ground black pepper, to taste
- 1 tablespoon unsalted butter or additional olive oil
- 1 small red onion, diced
- 2 cups kale, stems removed and leaves chopped
- 4 large eggs
- 1/4 cup grated Parmesan cheese (optional)

- Fresh parsley, chopped, for garnish

Directions:

1. Preheat your oven to 400°F (200°C). Toss the diced sweet potatoes with olive oil, smoked paprika, salt, and pepper on a baking sheet. Roast for 25-30 minutes, or until tender and golden, stirring halfway through.
2. Heat butter or olive oil in a large skillet over medium heat. Add the diced red onion and cook until soft, about 5 minutes.
3. Add the chopped kale to the skillet, stirring until the kale is wilted and tender, about 3-4 minutes.
4. Stir in the roasted sweet potatoes, mixing well with the kale and onion.
5. Create four wells in the hash and crack an egg into each. Cover the skillet and cook until the egg whites are set but the yolks are still runny, about 5 minutes.
6. Sprinkle with Parmesan cheese, if using, and garnish with fresh parsley. Serve immediately.

Nutritional Values:

- Calories: 290 (per serving)
- Protein: 10g
- Carbohydrates: 38g
- Fat: 12g
- Fiber: 6g

Caprese Stuffed Avocado

Ingredients:

- 2 large ripe avocados, halved and pits removed
- 1 cup cherry tomatoes, halved
- 4 ounces fresh mozzarella cheese, cubed
- 1/4 cup basil leaves, torn

- 2 tablespoons balsamic glaze
- Salt and freshly ground black pepper, to taste
- Extra virgin olive oil, for drizzling

Directions:

1. Use a spoon to scoop out a bit of each avocado half to create a larger well. Dice the scooped avocado and set aside.
2. In a bowl, combine the diced avocado, cherry tomatoes, mozzarella cubes, and torn basil. Season with salt and pepper to taste.
3. Spoon the tomato and mozzarella mixture back into the avocado wells, heaping it on top.
4. Drizzle with balsamic glaze and a bit of extra virgin olive oil before serving.

Nutritional Values:

- Calories: 320 (per half stuffed avocado)
- Protein: 12g
- Carbohydrates: 20g
- Fat: 24g
- Fiber: 7g

Pesto Pasta with Sun-Dried Tomatoes and Pine Nuts

Ingredients:

- 8 oz whole wheat spaghetti or your favorite pasta
- 1/2 cup basil pesto, homemade or store-bought
- 1/2 cup sun-dried tomatoes in oil, drained and chopped
- 1/3 cup pine nuts, toasted
- 1/4 cup Parmesan cheese, grated (optional)
- Fresh basil leaves, for garnish

- Salt and freshly ground black pepper, to taste

Directions:

1. Cook the pasta according to package instructions in a large pot of salted boiling water until al dente. Drain and return to the pot.
2. While the pasta is still warm, add the basil pesto and toss until the pasta is evenly coated.
3. Stir in the sun-dried tomatoes and toasted pine nuts, mixing well.
4. Season with salt and pepper to taste.
5. Serve the pasta garnished with grated Parmesan cheese and fresh basil leaves.

Nutritional Values:

- Calories: 420 (per serving)
- Protein: 12g
- Carbohydrates: 56g
- Fat: 18g
- Fiber: 8g

Grilled Vegetable and Goat Cheese Sandwich

Ingredients:

- 2 zucchinis, sliced lengthwise
- 1 red bell pepper, seeded and quartered
- 1 eggplant, sliced into rounds
- 2 tablespoons olive oil
- Salt and freshly ground black pepper, to taste
- 4 large slices of sourdough bread
- 4 ounces goat cheese, softened
- 1/4 cup red onion, thinly sliced

- 1 tablespoon balsamic vinegar
- A handful of arugula or spinach leaves

Directions:

1. Preheat your grill or grill pan over medium-high heat.
2. Brush the zucchini, bell pepper, and eggplant slices with olive oil and season with salt and pepper.
3. Grill the vegetables for 3-4 minutes on each side, or until tender and charred.
4. Toast the sourdough bread slices on the grill for about 1 minute on each side, or until lightly toasted.
5. Spread the goat cheese evenly on one side of each bread slice.
6. Layer the grilled vegetables and red onion slices on top of the goat cheese. Drizzle with balsamic vinegar and add a handful of arugula or spinach leaves.
7. Top with another slice of bread, goat cheese side down.
8. Cut each sandwich in half and serve immediately.

Nutritional Values:

- Calories: 380 (per sandwich)
- Protein: 14g
- Carbohydrates: 45g
- Fat: 18g
- Fiber: 6g

Beetroot and Feta Cheese Salad

Ingredients:

- 4 medium beetroots, peeled and diced
- 2 tablespoons olive oil
- Salt and freshly ground black pepper, to taste
- 1/2 cup walnuts, roughly chopped
- 2 cups mixed salad greens (such as arugula and spinach)

- 1/2 cup feta cheese, crumbled
- 2 tablespoons balsamic glaze

Directions:

1. Preheat the oven to 400°F (200°C). Toss the diced beetroots with olive oil, salt, and pepper on a baking sheet. Roast for 25-30 minutes, or until tender and slightly caramelized, stirring occasionally.
2. Toast the walnuts in a dry skillet over medium heat for 3-4 minutes, or until fragrant and lightly browned. Set aside to cool.
3. In a large bowl, combine the roasted beetroots, toasted walnuts, and mixed salad greens. Gently toss the ingredients.
4. Sprinkle the crumbled feta cheese over the salad.
5. Just before serving, drizzle the salad with balsamic glaze.
6. Serve immediately as a refreshing and colorful lunch option.

Nutritional Values:

- Calories: 290 (per serving)
- Protein: 7g
- Carbohydrates: 18g
- Fat: 21g
- Fiber: 4g

Spicy Black Bean Soup

Ingredients:

- 2 cans (15 oz each) black beans, rinsed and drained
- 2 tablespoons vegetable oil
- 1 onion, chopped
- 2 garlic cloves, minced
- 1 red bell pepper, chopped
- 1 teaspoon ground cumin
- 1/2 teaspoon chili powder

- 4 cups vegetable broth
- Juice of 1 lime
- Salt and freshly ground black pepper, to taste
- Sour cream, for serving (optional)
- Fresh cilantro, chopped, for garnish

Directions:

1. Heat the vegetable oil in a large pot over medium heat. Add the onion, garlic, and bell pepper, cooking until softened, about 5 minutes.
2. Stir in the ground cumin and chili powder, cooking for an additional minute until fragrant.
3. Add the black beans and vegetable broth. Bring to a boil, then reduce heat and simmer for 15 minutes.
4. Using an immersion blender, partially blend the soup to thicken it while leaving some beans whole for texture.
5. Stir in the lime juice and season with salt and pepper to taste.
6. Serve hot, topped with a dollop of sour cream (if using) and a sprinkle of fresh cilantro.

Nutritional Values:

- Calories: 210 (per serving without sour cream)
- Protein: 11g
- Carbohydrates: 34g
- Fat: 4g
- Fiber: 10g

Asian-Inspired Tofu Noodle Bowl

Ingredients:

- 8 oz rice noodles
- 14 oz firm tofu, pressed and cubed
- 2 tablespoons soy sauce
- 1 tablespoon sesame oil
- 1 tablespoon rice vinegar
- 1 teaspoon honey or maple syrup
- 1 carrot, julienned
- 1 cucumber, julienned
- 1 red bell pepper, thinly sliced
- 1/4 cup green onions, chopped
- 1/4 cup fresh cilantro, chopped
- 2 tablespoons peanuts, crushed
- Lime wedges, for serving

Directions:

1. Cook rice noodles according to package instructions, drain, and set aside.
2. In a bowl, whisk together soy sauce, sesame oil, rice vinegar, and honey or maple syrup. Add the tofu cubes and gently toss to coat. Let marinate for 10 minutes.
3. Heat a non-stick pan over medium heat and add the marinated tofu. Cook until all sides are golden brown, about 5-7 minutes.
4. In a large bowl, combine the cooked noodles, cooked tofu, carrot, cucumber, bell pepper, green onions, and cilantro. Toss gently to mix.
5. Divide the noodle mixture among serving bowls. Garnish with crushed peanuts and serve with lime wedges on the side.

Nutritional Values:

- Calories: 380 (per serving)

- Protein: 14g
- Carbohydrates: 56g
- Fat: 12g
- Fiber: 3g

Mediterranean Stuffed Bell Peppers

Ingredients:

- 4 large bell peppers, halved and seeds removed
- 1 cup quinoa, cooked
- 1 can (15 oz) chickpeas, rinsed and drained
- 1 cup cherry tomatoes, halved
- 1/2 cup Kalamata olives, pitted and chopped
- 1/2 cup crumbled feta cheese
- 1/4 cup red onion, finely chopped
- 1/4 cup fresh parsley, chopped
- 2 tablespoons olive oil
- Juice of 1 lemon
- Salt and freshly ground black pepper, to taste

Directions:

1. Preheat the oven to 375°F (190°C). Place the bell pepper halves in a baking dish, cut-side up.
2. In a large bowl, mix together the cooked quinoa, chickpeas, cherry tomatoes, olives, feta cheese, red onion, and parsley.
3. Drizzle with olive oil and lemon juice, season with salt and pepper, and toss to combine.
4. Stuff the bell pepper halves with the quinoa mixture, pressing lightly to pack it in.
5. Cover the baking dish with foil and bake for about 25-30 minutes, or until the peppers are tender.
6. Serve the stuffed peppers warm, optionally garnished with additional fresh parsley or feta.

Nutritional Values:

- Calories: 320 (per serving)
- Protein: 10g
- Carbohydrates: 45g
- Fat: 12g
- Fiber: 8g

Warm Spinach and Artichoke Tart

Ingredients:

- 1 sheet puff pastry, thawed
- 1 tablespoon olive oil
- 2 garlic cloves, minced
- 4 cups fresh spinach
- 1 can (14 oz) artichoke hearts, drained and chopped
- 1/2 cup ricotta cheese
- 1/4 cup grated Parmesan cheese
- Salt and freshly ground black pepper, to taste
- 1 egg, beaten, for egg wash

Directions:

1. Preheat your oven to 400°F (200°C). Roll out the puff pastry on a lightly floured surface and place it on a baking sheet lined with parchment paper.
2. In a large skillet, heat the olive oil over medium heat. Add the garlic and sauté for 1 minute until fragrant. Add the spinach and cook until wilted. Remove from heat.
3. Stir in the chopped artichoke hearts, ricotta, and Parmesan cheese into the spinach mixture. Season with salt and pepper.
4. Spread the spinach and artichoke mixture over the center of the puff pastry, leaving a 1-inch border around the edges.

5. Fold the edges of the puff pastry over the filling, slightly overlapping and pressing to seal. Brush the edges with egg wash.
6. Bake for 20-25 minutes, or until the pastry is golden brown and puffed.
7. Let cool for a few minutes before slicing and serving.

Nutritional Values:

- Calories: 330 (per serving)
- Protein: 9g
- Carbohydrates: 28g
- Fat: 20g
- Fiber: 2g

Classic Tomato Basil Soup

Ingredients:

- 2 tablespoons olive oil
- 1 onion, diced
- 3 garlic cloves, minced
- 2 cans (14 oz each) diced tomatoes, undrained
- 2 cups vegetable broth
- 1/2 cup fresh basil leaves, chopped
- 1 teaspoon sugar
- Salt and freshly ground black pepper, to taste
- 1/2 cup heavy cream or coconut milk (for a vegan option)
- Fresh basil leaves, for garnish

Directions:

1. In a large pot, heat the olive oil over medium heat. Add the onion and garlic, and sauté until soft and translucent, about 5 minutes.

2. Add the diced tomatoes (with their juice), vegetable broth, chopped basil, sugar, salt, and pepper. Bring to a boil, then reduce heat and simmer for 20 minutes.
3. Use an immersion blender to puree the soup until smooth (or carefully transfer to a blender in batches).
4. Stir in the heavy cream or coconut milk and heat through, without boiling.
5. Taste and adjust seasoning as necessary.
6. Serve hot, garnished with fresh basil leaves.

Nutritional Values:

- Calories: 200 (per serving)
- Protein: 3g
- Carbohydrates: 16g
- Fat: 14g
- Fiber: 3g

Lemon Herb Couscous Salad

Ingredients:

- 1 cup couscous
- 1 1/4 cups vegetable broth
- Zest and juice of 1 lemon
- 2 tablespoons olive oil
- 1/2 cup cherry tomatoes, halved
- 1/2 cucumber, diced
- 1/4 cup red onion, finely chopped
- 1/4 cup kalamata olives, sliced
- 1/4 cup fresh parsley, chopped
- 1/4 cup fresh mint, chopped
- Salt and freshly ground black pepper, to taste
- Feta cheese, crumbled (optional)

Directions:

1. Bring the vegetable broth to a boil in a medium saucepan. Add the couscous, cover, and remove from heat. Let stand for 5 minutes, then fluff with a fork.
2. In a large bowl, whisk together the lemon zest, lemon juice, and olive oil. Add the cooked couscous, cherry tomatoes, cucumber, red onion, olives, parsley, and mint. Toss to combine.
3. Season with salt and pepper to taste. Garnish with crumbled feta cheese if desired.
4. Serve chilled or at room temperature.

Nutritional Values:

- Calories: 210 (per serving, without feta)
- Protein: 6g
- Carbohydrates: 33g
- Fat: 7g
- Fiber: 3g

Smoky Red Pepper and Chickpea Soup

Ingredients:

- 2 tablespoons olive oil
- 1 onion, chopped
- 2 garlic cloves, minced
- 2 teaspoons smoked paprika
- 1 can (15 oz) chickpeas, drained and rinsed
- 1 jar (12 oz) roasted red peppers, drained and chopped
- 4 cups vegetable broth
- Salt and freshly ground black pepper, to taste
- Sour cream or Greek yogurt, for serving (optional)
- Fresh parsley, chopped, for garnish

Directions:

1. Heat the olive oil in a large pot over medium heat. Add the onion and garlic, cooking until soft and translucent.
2. Stir in the smoked paprika, chickpeas, and roasted red peppers, cooking for an additional 2 minutes.
3. Add the vegetable broth and bring to a simmer. Cook for 15 minutes, allowing the flavors to meld.
4. Use an immersion blender to puree the soup until smooth. Season with salt and pepper to taste.
5. Serve hot, topped with a dollop of sour cream or Greek yogurt and a sprinkle of fresh parsley.

Nutritional Values:

- Calories: 190 (per serving, without sour cream/yogurt)
- Protein: 7g
- Carbohydrates: 28g
- Fat: 6g
- Fiber: 6g

Dinner Recipes

Roasted Butternut Squash Risotto

Ingredients:

- 1 butternut squash, peeled and cubed (about 3 cups)
- 3 tablespoons olive oil, divided
- Salt and freshly ground black pepper, to taste
- 1 small onion, finely chopped
- 2 cloves garlic, minced
- 1 cup Arborio rice
- 1/2 cup dry white wine
- 4 cups vegetable broth, kept warm
- 1/2 cup Parmesan cheese, grated
- Fresh sage, chopped, for garnish

Directions:

1. Preheat the oven to 425°F (220°C). Toss the butternut squash cubes with 2 tablespoons of olive oil, salt, and pepper. Spread on a baking sheet and roast for 25-30 minutes, or until tender and caramelized, stirring halfway through.
2. In a large skillet or saucepan, heat the remaining tablespoon of olive oil over medium heat. Add the onion and garlic, sautéing until soft and translucent.
3. Stir in the Arborio rice, toasting for about 1 minute until slightly translucent around the edges. Pour in the white wine, stirring continuously, until mostly absorbed.
4. Begin adding the warm vegetable broth, one ladle at a time, stirring frequently. Wait until the liquid is almost fully absorbed before adding more. Continue this process until the rice is creamy and cooked through, about 20 minutes.
5. Gently fold the roasted butternut squash into the risotto. Stir in the Parmesan cheese.

6. Serve hot, garnished with fresh sage and additional Parmesan if desired.

Nutritional Values:

- Calories: 360 (per serving)
- Protein: 9g
- Carbohydrates: 53g
- Fat: 12g
- Fiber: 4g

Stuffed Portobello Mushrooms with Spinach and Goat Cheese

Ingredients:

- 4 large Portobello mushroom caps, stems and gills removed
- 2 tablespoons olive oil, plus extra for brushing
- Salt and freshly ground black pepper, to taste
- 2 cups spinach, chopped
- 1/4 cup red onion, finely chopped
- 2 cloves garlic, minced
- 1/2 cup goat cheese, crumbled
- 1/4 cup breadcrumbs
- 2 tablespoons fresh thyme, chopped
- Balsamic glaze, for drizzling

Directions:

1. Preheat the oven to 375°F (190°C). Brush both sides of the mushroom caps with olive oil and season with salt and pepper. Place them stem-side up on a baking sheet and bake for 10 minutes.

2. Meanwhile, heat 2 tablespoons of olive oil in a skillet over medium heat. Add the spinach, red onion, and garlic, cooking until the spinach is wilted and the onion is soft.
3. Remove the skillet from the heat. Stir in the goat cheese, breadcrumbs, and thyme until well combined.
4. Remove the mushrooms from the oven. Fill each cap with the spinach and goat cheese mixture, pressing gently to compact.
5. Return the mushrooms to the oven and bake for an additional 15 minutes, or until the topping is golden and the mushrooms are tender.
6. Serve immediately, drizzled with balsamic glaze.

Nutritional Values:

- Calories: 250 (per serving)
- Protein: 10g
- Carbohydrates: 18g
- Fat: 16g
- Fiber: 3g

Eggplant Parmesan Tower

Ingredients:

- 2 large eggplants, sliced into 1/2-inch rounds
- Salt
- 3 tablespoons olive oil
- 2 cups marinara sauce
- 1 cup fresh mozzarella, sliced
- 1/2 cup grated Parmesan cheese
- 1/4 cup fresh basil leaves, plus more for garnish
- 1/2 cup breadcrumbs
- 1/2 teaspoon garlic powder
- Freshly ground black pepper, to taste

Directions:

1. Preheat your oven to 400°F (200°C). Lay the eggplant slices on a baking sheet, sprinkle lightly with salt, and let them sit for about 15 minutes to draw out moisture. Pat dry with paper towels.
2. Brush both sides of the eggplant slices with olive oil and place them back on the baking sheet. Bake for 20 minutes, flipping halfway through, until golden and softened.
3. In a small bowl, mix breadcrumbs with garlic powder and a pinch of salt and pepper.
4. On a baking dish, start to build the towers by placing a spoonful of marinara on the bottom, then layering eggplant, a slice of mozzarella, a sprinkle of Parmesan, some basil leaves, and a little of the breadcrumb mixture. Repeat the layers until you have 2-3 layers per tower, finishing with cheese on top.
5. Bake in the oven for 10-15 minutes, or until the cheese is bubbly and golden.
6. Serve hot, garnished with fresh basil leaves.

Nutritional Values:

- Calories: 310 (per serving)
- Protein: 14g
- Carbohydrates: 24g
- Fat: 19g
- Fiber: 6g

Quinoa Stuffed Bell Peppers

Ingredients:

- 4 large bell peppers, tops removed and seeded
- 1 cup quinoa, cooked
- 1 tablespoon olive oil
- 1 small onion, diced

- 2 cloves garlic, minced
- 1 zucchini, diced
- 1 cup black beans, drained and rinsed
- 1 cup corn kernels (fresh or frozen and thawed)
- 1 teaspoon ground cumin
- 1/2 teaspoon chili powder
- 1 cup shredded cheddar cheese, divided
- Salt and freshly ground black pepper, to taste
- Fresh cilantro, for garnish

Directions:

1. Preheat your oven to 350°F (175°C). Place the bell peppers in a baking dish, cut-side up.
2. Heat olive oil in a skillet over medium heat. Add onion and garlic, cooking until softened. Add zucchini, black beans, corn, cumin, and chili powder. Cook for 5 minutes until fragrant.
3. Remove from heat. Stir in the cooked quinoa and half of the cheddar cheese. Season with salt and pepper.
4. Stuff each bell pepper with the quinoa mixture, packing tightly. Top with the remaining cheddar cheese.
5. Cover the baking dish with foil and bake for 30 minutes. Uncover and bake for an additional 10 minutes, or until the cheese is golden and bubbly.
6. Garnish with fresh cilantro before serving.

Nutritional Values:

- Calories: 365 (per stuffed pepper)
- Protein: 16g
- Carbohydrates: 45g
- Fat: 15g
- Fiber: 8g

Eggplant Parmesan Tower

Ingredients:

- 2 large eggplants, sliced into 1/2-inch rounds
- Salt
- 3 tablespoons olive oil
- 2 cups marinara sauce
- 1 cup fresh mozzarella, sliced
- 1/2 cup grated Parmesan cheese
- 1/4 cup fresh basil leaves, plus more for garnish
- 1/2 cup breadcrumbs
- 1/2 teaspoon garlic powder
- Freshly ground black pepper, to taste

Directions:

7. Preheat your oven to 400°F (200°C). Lay the eggplant slices on a baking sheet, sprinkle lightly with salt, and let them sit for about 15 minutes to draw out moisture. Pat dry with paper towels.
8. Brush both sides of the eggplant slices with olive oil and place them back on the baking sheet. Bake for 20 minutes, flipping halfway through, until golden and softened.
9. In a small bowl, mix breadcrumbs with garlic powder and a pinch of salt and pepper.
10. On a baking dish, start to build the towers by placing a spoonful of marinara on the bottom, then layering eggplant, a slice of mozzarella, a sprinkle of Parmesan, some basil leaves, and a little of the breadcrumb mixture. Repeat the layers until you have 2-3 layers per tower, finishing with cheese on top.
11. Bake in the oven for 10-15 minutes, or until the cheese is bubbly and golden.
12. Serve hot, garnished with fresh basil leaves.

Nutritional Values:

- Calories: 310 (per serving)
- Protein: 14g
- Carbohydrates: 24g
- Fat: 19g
- Fiber: 6g

Garden Vegetable Lasagna

Ingredients:

- 9 lasagna noodles, cooked al dente
- 1 tablespoon olive oil
- 1 small zucchini, thinly sliced
- 1 small yellow squash, thinly sliced
- 1 red bell pepper, thinly sliced
- 1 cup spinach, roughly chopped
- 2 cups ricotta cheese
- 1 egg
- 1/4 cup fresh basil, chopped
- 2 cups marinara sauce
- 2 cups shredded mozzarella cheese
- 1/2 cup grated Parmesan cheese
- Salt and freshly ground black pepper, to taste

Directions:

1. Preheat the oven to 375°F (190°C). Heat olive oil in a skillet over medium heat and sauté zucchini, squash, bell pepper until tender. Add spinach until wilted. Set aside.
2. Mix ricotta, egg, basil, salt, and pepper in a bowl.
3. Spread a layer of marinara sauce in a 9x13 inch baking dish. Lay three noodles over sauce.
4. Layer with half of the ricotta mixture, half the vegetable mixture, a third of the mozzarella, and a third of the Parmesan.

Repeat layers, ending with noodles, marinara, mozzarella, and Parmesan.
5. Cover with foil and bake for 25 minutes. Remove foil and bake for another 25 minutes until golden. Let stand for 10 minutes before serving.

Nutritional Values:

- Calories: 450 (per serving)
- Protein: 25g
- Carbohydrates: 35g
- Fat: 25g
- Fiber: 3g

Cauliflower Steak with Chimichurri Sauce

Ingredients:

- 2 large heads cauliflower
- 3 tablespoons olive oil, divided
- Salt and freshly ground black pepper, to taste
- **For the Chimichurri Sauce:**
    - 1 cup fresh parsley, finely chopped
    - 1/4 cup fresh cilantro, finely chopped
    - 1/4 cup olive oil
    - 2 tablespoons red wine vinegar
    - 2 garlic cloves, minced
    - 1/2 teaspoon red pepper flakes
    - Salt and pepper, to taste

Directions:

1. Preheat the oven to 400°F (200°C). Slice cauliflower into 1-inch steaks. Brush with olive oil, season with salt and pepper, and sear in a hot pan, 2 minutes each side.

2. Transfer to baking sheet and roast until tender, about 15 minutes.
3. For chimichurri, mix parsley, cilantro, olive oil, vinegar, garlic, red pepper flakes, salt, and pepper in a bowl.
4. Serve cauliflower steaks with chimichurri sauce drizzled on top.

Nutritional Values:

- Calories: 280 (per serving)
- Protein: 5g
- Carbohydrates: 12g
- Fat: 24g
- Fiber: 5g

Wild Mushroom and Truffle Oil Risotto

Ingredients:

- 1 cup Arborio rice
- 2 tablespoons olive oil
- 1 small onion, finely chopped
- 2 cloves garlic, minced
- 1/2 pound wild mushrooms, cleaned and sliced (such as shiitake, oyster, and cremini)
- 4 cups vegetable broth, warmed
- 1/2 cup dry white wine
- 2 tablespoons truffle oil
- 1/2 cup grated Parmesan cheese
- Salt and freshly ground black pepper, to taste
- Fresh parsley, chopped, for garnish

Directions:

1. In a large pan, heat the olive oil over medium heat. Add the onion and garlic, sautéing until translucent.

2. Add the mushrooms and cook until they begin to release their moisture and brown slightly.
3. Stir in the Arborio rice, toasting it until the edges become slightly translucent.
4. Pour in the white wine, stirring continuously until the wine is mostly absorbed.
5. Begin adding the warm vegetable broth, one ladle at a time, allowing the rice to absorb the liquid before adding more. Continue stirring often.
6. Once the rice is creamy and al dente, remove from heat. Stir in the truffle oil and grated Parmesan. Season with salt and pepper to taste.
7. Serve garnished with fresh parsley and additional Parmesan if desired.

Nutritional Values:

- Calories: 380 per serving
- Protein: 10g
- Carbohydrates: 53g
- Fat: 14g
- Fiber: 2g

Balsamic Glazed Caprese Skewers

Ingredients:

- 16 cherry tomatoes
- 16 small mozzarella balls (bocconcini)
- 16 fresh basil leaves
- 2 tablespoons balsamic glaze
- 2 tablespoons olive oil
- Salt and freshly ground black pepper, to taste
- 8 wooden skewers

Directions:

1. Thread each skewer with a cherry tomato, a basil leaf (folded if large), and a mozzarella ball. Repeat once more on each skewer so there are two sets of each ingredient per skewer.
2. Arrange the skewers on a platter. Drizzle with olive oil and balsamic glaze.
3. Season with salt and pepper to taste.
4. Serve immediately, or let sit for up to an hour to allow the flavors to meld together.

Nutritional Values:

- Calories: 150 per serving (2 skewers)
- Protein: 8g
- Carbohydrates: 4g
- Fat: 11g
- Fiber: 1g

Spinach and Ricotta Stuffed Shells

Ingredients:

- 24 jumbo pasta shells
- 2 tablespoons olive oil
- 2 cups ricotta cheese
- 2 cups fresh spinach, chopped
- 1 cup grated mozzarella cheese, divided
- 1/2 cup grated Parmesan cheese, plus extra for serving
- 1 egg, beaten
- Salt and freshly ground black pepper, to taste
- 2 cups marinara sauce
- Fresh basil, for garnish

Directions:

1. Preheat your oven to 375°F (190°C). Cook the pasta shells according to package instructions until al dente. Drain and set aside to cool.
2. In a skillet, heat olive oil over medium heat. Add spinach and cook until wilted. Let it cool.
3. In a mixing bowl, combine ricotta cheese, cooked spinach, 1/2 cup mozzarella cheese, Parmesan cheese, and the beaten egg. Season with salt and pepper.
4. Spread a thin layer of marinara sauce at the bottom of a baking dish.
5. Stuff each pasta shell with the ricotta-spinach mixture and place in the baking dish.
6. Pour the remaining marinara sauce over the stuffed shells. Sprinkle with the remaining mozzarella cheese.
7. Cover with foil and bake for 25 minutes. Remove foil and bake for an additional 10 minutes, until cheese is bubbly and golden.
8. Serve garnished with fresh basil and additional Parmesan cheese.

Nutritional Values:

- Calories: 350 per serving (4 shells)
- Protein: 18g
- Carbohydrates: 32g
- Fat: 18g
- Fiber: 2g

Roasted Vegetable Tart

Ingredients:

- 1 sheet puff pastry, thawed
- 1 small zucchini, thinly sliced
- 1 small yellow squash, thinly sliced
- 1 red bell pepper, thinly sliced
- 1/2 red onion, thinly sliced
- 2 tablespoons olive oil
- Salt and freshly ground black pepper, to taste
- 1/2 cup goat cheese, crumbled
- 1/4 cup fresh basil leaves
- Balsamic glaze, for drizzling

Directions:

1. Preheat your oven to 400°F (200°C). Roll out the puff pastry on a baking sheet lined with parchment paper.
2. Toss zucchini, yellow squash, red bell pepper, and red onion with olive oil, salt, and pepper.
3. Arrange the vegetables evenly over the puff pastry, leaving a 1-inch border around the edges.
4. Fold the edges of the puff pastry over the vegetables, pressing gently to seal.
5. Sprinkle the crumbled goat cheese over the vegetables.
6. Bake for 25-30 minutes, until the pastry is golden and the vegetables are tender.
7. Garnish with fresh basil leaves and drizzle with balsamic glaze before serving.

Nutritional Values:

- Calories: 320 per serving (1/6 of tart)
- Protein: 7g
- Carbohydrates: 28g

- Fat: 20g
- Fiber: 3g

Creamy Polenta with Roasted Mushrooms

Ingredients:

- 1 cup polenta (cornmeal)
- 4 cups vegetable broth
- 2 tablespoons unsalted butter
- 1/2 cup grated Parmesan cheese
- Salt and freshly ground black pepper, to taste
- 2 tablespoons olive oil
- 1 pound mixed mushrooms (such as shiitake, cremini, and portobello), sliced
- 2 garlic cloves, minced
- 1/4 cup fresh thyme leaves
- Additional grated Parmesan and fresh thyme for garnish

Directions:

1. In a medium saucepan, bring the vegetable broth to a boil. Gradually whisk in the polenta, reduce the heat to low, and cook, stirring frequently, until thickened and creamy, about 20-30 minutes.
2. Remove from heat and stir in the butter and grated Parmesan. Season with salt and pepper to taste. Cover and set aside.
3. Preheat the oven to 425°F (220°C). Toss the sliced mushrooms with olive oil, minced garlic, thyme, salt, and pepper. Spread on a baking sheet in a single layer.
4. Roast the mushrooms for 20-25 minutes, or until golden and tender, stirring halfway through.
5. Serve the creamy polenta topped with the roasted mushrooms, garnished with additional Parmesan and thyme.

Nutritional Values:

- Calories: 380 per serving
- Protein: 12g
- Carbohydrates: 45g
- Fat: 18g
- Fiber: 4g

Lemon Garlic Pasta with Broccoli

Ingredients:

- 8 oz spaghetti or linguine
- 2 tablespoons olive oil
- 3 garlic cloves, thinly sliced
- 1 broccoli crown, cut into florets
- Zest and juice of 1 lemon
- 1/2 teaspoon red pepper flakes (optional)
- Salt and freshly ground black pepper, to taste
- 1/4 cup grated Parmesan cheese
- Fresh parsley, chopped, for garnish

Directions:

1. Cook the pasta according to package instructions until al dente. Reserve 1/2 cup of pasta water, then drain and set aside.
2. In the same pot, heat olive oil over medium heat. Add garlic and sauté until golden, about 1 minute.
3. Add broccoli florets, lemon zest, lemon juice, red pepper flakes (if using), salt, and pepper. Cook, stirring occasionally, until the broccoli is tender, about 5-7 minutes.
4. Return the cooked pasta to the pot. Add a splash of the reserved pasta water to help the sauce coat the pasta evenly. Heat through, stirring well.
5. Serve the pasta sprinkled with grated Parmesan and garnished with fresh parsley.

Nutritional Values:

- Calories: 350 per serving
- Protein: 12g
- Carbohydrates: 52g
- Fat: 10g
- Fiber: 4g

Zesty Thai Green Curry with Vegetables

Ingredients:

- 1 tablespoon coconut oil
- 2 tablespoons Thai green curry paste
- 1 can (14 oz) coconut milk
- 1 cup vegetable broth
- 1 tablespoon soy sauce
- 1 tablespoon sugar
- 2 cups mixed vegetables (such as bell peppers, carrots, and snap peas), sliced
- 1 cup broccoli florets
- 1/2 cup bamboo shoots, drained
- 1/2 cup fresh basil leaves
- Juice of 1 lime
- Salt, to taste
- Cooked jasmine rice, for serving

Directions:

1. Heat the coconut oil in a large skillet over medium heat. Add the green curry paste and sauté for 1 minute until fragrant.
2. Stir in the coconut milk, vegetable broth, soy sauce, and sugar, bringing the mixture to a simmer.

3. Add the mixed vegetables and broccoli florets to the skillet. Cook for about 5-7 minutes until the vegetables are tender but still crisp.
4. Mix in the bamboo shoots, basil leaves, and lime juice. Season with salt to taste.
5. Serve the curry hot over cooked jasmine rice, garnished with additional basil if desired.

Nutritional Values:

- Calories: 320 per serving (excluding rice)
- Protein: 4g
- Carbohydrates: 24g
- Fat: 24g
- Fiber: 3g

Grilled Vegetable and Goat Cheese Panzanella

Ingredients:

- 4 cups of day-old bread, cubed
- 3 tablespoons olive oil, divided
- 2 bell peppers (1 red, 1 yellow), sliced
- 1 zucchini, sliced lengthwise
- 1 red onion, sliced into rings
- 2 tablespoons balsamic vinegar
- 1/2 cup cherry tomatoes, halved
- 1/4 cup fresh basil leaves, torn
- 1/3 cup goat cheese, crumbled
- Salt and freshly ground black pepper, to taste

Directions:

1. Preheat your grill to medium-high heat. Toss the bread cubes with 1 tablespoon of olive oil, and grill until crispy and golden brown. Set aside.
2. Brush the bell peppers, zucchini, and red onion with another tablespoon of olive oil. Grill the vegetables until charred and tender, turning occasionally.
3. In a large bowl, whisk together the remaining olive oil and balsamic vinegar. Season with salt and pepper.
4. Add the grilled vegetables, cherry tomatoes, and grilled bread cubes to the bowl. Toss to coat everything in the dressing.
5. Just before serving, fold in the fresh basil and crumbled goat cheese.
6. Serve immediately, enjoying the blend of warm grilled vegetables with the cool, creamy goat cheese.

Nutritional Values:

- Calories: 290 per serving
- Protein: 9g
- Carbohydrates: 32g
- Fat: 15g
- Fiber: 4g

Smoky Beet Burgers

Ingredients:

- 2 large beets, grated
- 1 can (15 oz) black beans, rinsed and drained
- 1/2 cup breadcrumbs
- 1/4 cup finely chopped red onion
- 2 cloves garlic, minced
- 1 teaspoon smoked paprika
- 1/2 teaspoon ground cumin

- Salt and freshly ground black pepper, to taste
- 2 tablespoons olive oil, for cooking
- Whole wheat burger buns, for serving
- Lettuce, tomato slices, and avocado, for topping

Directions:

1. In a large bowl, mash the black beans until mostly smooth. Stir in the grated beets, breadcrumbs, red onion, garlic, smoked paprika, cumin, salt, and pepper until well combined.
2. Form the mixture into burger patties.
3. Heat olive oil in a large skillet over medium heat. Cook the patties for about 5 minutes on each side, or until they are well browned and heated through.
4. Serve the beet burgers on whole wheat buns, topped with lettuce, tomato, and avocado slices.

Nutritional Values:

- Calories: 320 per serving (1 burger without bun and toppings)
- Protein: 9g
- Carbohydrates: 45g
- Fat: 12g
- Fiber: 10g

Butternut Squash and Sage Gnocchi

Ingredients:

- 2 cups mashed butternut squash (from about 1 small squash)
- 2 cups all-purpose flour, plus more for dusting
- 1/4 cup grated Parmesan cheese
- 2 tablespoons fresh sage, chopped, plus whole leaves for garnish
- 1/4 teaspoon nutmeg
- Salt and freshly ground black pepper, to taste
- 4 tablespoons unsalted butter

- Salted water, for boiling

Directions:

1. In a large bowl, mix together the mashed butternut squash, flour, Parmesan cheese, chopped sage, nutmeg, salt, and pepper until a dough forms.
2. On a floured surface, divide the dough and roll into long ropes. Cut into 1-inch pieces to form gnocchi.
3. Bring a large pot of salted water to a boil. Cook the gnocchi in batches until they float to the surface, about 2-3 minutes. Remove with a slotted spoon and set aside.
4. In a large skillet, melt the butter over medium heat. Add whole sage leaves and cook until the butter starts to brown and the sage is crispy.
5. Add the boiled gnocchi to the skillet, tossing to coat in the sage butter.
6. Serve immediately, garnished with additional Parmesan and crispy sage leaves.

Nutritional Values:

- Calories: 390 per serving
- Protein: 10g
- Carbohydrates: 58g
- Fat: 14g
- Fiber: 4g

Walnut and Lentil Bolognese

Ingredients:

- 1 cup green lentils, rinsed
- 2 tablespoons olive oil
- 1 onion, finely chopped

- 2 carrots, peeled and diced
- 2 celery stalks, diced
- 3 garlic cloves, minced
- 1 cup walnuts, finely chopped
- 2 tablespoons tomato paste
- 1 can (28 oz) crushed tomatoes
- 1 teaspoon dried oregano
- 1 teaspoon dried basil
- Salt and freshly ground black pepper, to taste
- 1/2 cup red wine (optional)
- 12 oz spaghetti or your choice of pasta
- Fresh basil, for garnish
- Grated Parmesan cheese, for serving

Directions:

1. Cook lentils in a pot of boiling water until tender, about 20-25 minutes. Drain and set aside.
2. Heat olive oil in a large skillet over medium heat. Add onion, carrots, celery, and garlic. Cook until softened, about 8 minutes.
3. Stir in the walnuts and tomato paste, cooking for another 2 minutes.
4. Add the crushed tomatoes, oregano, basil, cooked lentils, salt, pepper, and red wine if using. Simmer on low heat for 25-30 minutes, stirring occasionally.
5. Meanwhile, cook pasta according to package directions until al dente. Drain.
6. Serve the walnut and lentil bolognese sauce over the pasta, garnished with fresh basil and grated Parmesan cheese.

Nutritional Values:

- Calories: 420 per serving
- Protein: 18g
- Carbohydrates: 56g
- Fat: 14g
- Fiber: 12g

Chickpea and Spinach Stuffed Portobello Mushrooms

Ingredients:

- 4 large Portobello mushroom caps, stems and gills removed
- 2 tablespoons olive oil, divided
- Salt and freshly ground black pepper, to taste
- 1 can (15 oz) chickpeas, drained and rinsed
- 2 cups fresh spinach, roughly chopped
- 1/2 cup feta cheese, crumbled
- 2 garlic cloves, minced
- 1 teaspoon smoked paprika
- Juice of 1 lemon
- Fresh parsley, for garnish

Directions:

1. Preheat the oven to 375°F (190°C). Brush Portobello mushrooms with 1 tablespoon of olive oil and season with salt and pepper. Place on a baking sheet, cap-side down, and bake for 10 minutes.
2. Meanwhile, in a skillet, heat the remaining olive oil over medium heat. Add garlic and sauté until fragrant.
3. Add chickpeas, spinach, smoked paprika, and lemon juice. Cook until the spinach is wilted.
4. Stir in the feta cheese, cooking until just melted.
5. Remove the mushrooms from the oven and spoon the chickpea and spinach mixture into each cap.
6. Return to the oven and bake for an additional 10-15 minutes, until the mushrooms are tender and the filling is hot.
7. Serve garnished with fresh parsley.

Nutritional Values:

- Calories: 290 per serving
- Protein: 12g
- Carbohydrates: 24g
- **Sweet Potato and Black Bean Tacos**
- Fat: 18g
- Fiber: 6g

Sweet Potato and Black Bean Tacos

Ingredients:

- 2 large sweet potatoes, peeled and diced
- 1 tablespoon olive oil
- 1 teaspoon chili powder
- 1/2 teaspoon cumin
- Salt and pepper, to taste
- 1 can (15 oz) black beans, drained and rinsed
- 8 small corn tortillas
- 1 avocado, sliced
- 1/4 cup fresh cilantro, chopped
- Lime wedges, for serving
- 1/2 cup sour cream, for serving (optional)

Directions:

1. Preheat the oven to 425°F (220°C). Toss the diced sweet potatoes with olive oil, chili powder, cumin, salt, and pepper on a baking sheet. Roast for 25-30 minutes, until tender and slightly caramelized.
2. Warm the black beans in a pan over medium heat. Season with a pinch of salt and pepper.
3. Heat the corn tortillas according to package instructions, either in the microwave or over an open flame for a charred effect.

4. Assemble the tacos by placing a spoonful of black beans on each tortilla, followed by roasted sweet potatoes. Top with avocado slices and a sprinkle of cilantro.
5. Serve with lime wedges and a dollop of sour cream, if desired.

Nutritional Values:

- Calories: 320 per serving (2 tacos)
- Protein: 9g
- Carbohydrates: 50g
- Fat: 11g
- Fiber: 12g

Roasted Red Pepper Pasta

Ingredients:

- 12 oz fettuccine or spaghetti
- 2 tablespoons olive oil
- 2 garlic cloves, minced
- 1 jar (12 oz) roasted red peppers, drained and chopped
- 1 cup heavy cream or coconut milk for a vegan option
- 1/2 teaspoon red pepper flakes
- Salt and freshly ground black pepper, to taste
- 1/2 cup grated Parmesan cheese, plus more for serving (optional for vegan)
- Fresh basil leaves, for garnish

Directions:

1. Cook the pasta according to package instructions until al dente. Drain and set aside, reserving 1 cup of pasta water.
2. In a large skillet, heat the olive oil over medium heat. Add the minced garlic and cook until fragrant, about 1 minute.
3. Add the chopped roasted red peppers and cook for another 2-3 minutes.

4. Stir in the heavy cream (or coconut milk), red pepper flakes, salt, and pepper. Bring to a simmer.
5. Reduce the heat and blend the sauce using an immersion blender until smooth. If the sauce is too thick, add reserved pasta water until desired consistency is reached.
6. Add the cooked pasta to the sauce, tossing to coat. Stir in the grated Parmesan cheese until melted and smooth.
7. Serve hot, garnished with fresh basil leaves and additional Parmesan cheese, if desired.

Nutritional Values:

- Calories: 550 per serving
- Protein: 17g
- Carbohydrates: 67g
- Fat: 25g
- Fiber: 4g

Snacks and Sides

Crispy Baked Zucchini Fries

Ingredients:

- 2 medium zucchinis, cut into 3-inch sticks
- 1/2 cup all-purpose flour
- 2 large eggs, beaten
- 1 cup breadcrumbs
- 1/2 cup grated Parmesan cheese
- 1 teaspoon garlic powder
- Salt and freshly ground black pepper, to taste
- Cooking spray

Directions:

1. Preheat the oven to 425°F (220°C). Line a baking sheet with parchment paper and lightly spray with cooking spray.
2. Place flour, eggs, and breadcrumbs mixed with Parmesan cheese and garlic powder in three separate shallow dishes. Season each with salt and pepper.
3. Dredge each zucchini stick in flour, dip into eggs, then coat with the breadcrumb mixture. Place on the prepared baking sheet.
4. Spray the coated zucchini sticks lightly with cooking spray. Bake for 20-25 minutes, until golden brown and crispy.
5. Serve warm with your favorite dipping sauce.

Nutritional Values:

- Calories: 180 per serving (about 6 fries)
- Protein: 8g
- Carbohydrates: 20g
- Fat: 8g
- Fiber: 2g

Avocado and Chickpea Salad

Ingredients:

- 1 can (15 oz) chickpeas, rinsed and drained
- 2 ripe avocados, diced
- 1/2 red onion, finely chopped
- 1/4 cup fresh cilantro, chopped
- Juice of 1 lime
- 2 tablespoons olive oil
- Salt and freshly ground black pepper, to taste
- Chili flakes (optional), to taste

Directions:

1. In a large bowl, combine chickpeas, diced avocados, red onion, and cilantro.
2. In a small bowl, whisk together lime juice, olive oil, salt, pepper, and chili flakes if using.
3. Pour the dressing over the salad and gently toss to combine, being careful not to mash the avocados.
4. Adjust seasoning if necessary. Serve immediately, or chill in the refrigerator for 30 minutes before serving to enhance the flavors.

Nutritional Values:

- Calories: 250 per serving
- Protein: 7g
- Carbohydrates: 24g
- Fat: 15g
- Fiber: 8g

Sweet Potato Hummus

Ingredients:

- 1 large sweet potato, peeled and cubed
- 1 can (15 oz) chickpeas, rinsed and drained
- 3 tablespoons tahini
- 2 garlic cloves, minced
- Juice of 1 lemon
- 2 tablespoons olive oil
- 1/2 teaspoon smoked paprika
- Salt and freshly ground black pepper, to taste
- Water, as needed for consistency
- Fresh parsley, for garnish

Directions:

1. Steam or boil the sweet potato cubes until tender, about 15-20 minutes. Let cool.
2. In a food processor, combine the cooked sweet potato, chickpeas, tahini, garlic, lemon juice, olive oil, smoked paprika, salt, and pepper. Blend until smooth.
3. If the hummus is too thick, add water, one tablespoon at a time, until you reach your desired consistency.
4. Taste and adjust seasoning as needed.
5. Transfer to a serving bowl, drizzle with a little more olive oil, and garnish with fresh parsley.
6. Serve with vegetable sticks, pita chips, or as a spread on sandwiches.

Nutritional Values:

- Calories: 160 per serving (1/4 cup)
- Protein: 5g
- Carbohydrates: 20g

- Fat: 7g
- Fiber: 4g

Roasted Brussels Sprouts with Balsamic Glaze

Ingredients:

- 1 lb Brussels sprouts, trimmed and halved
- 2 tablespoons olive oil
- Salt and freshly ground black pepper, to taste
- 3 tablespoons balsamic vinegar
- 2 teaspoons honey or maple syrup for a vegan option
- 1/4 cup pecans, roughly chopped (optional)
- Grated Parmesan cheese, for serving (optional)

Directions:

1. Preheat the oven to 400°F (200°C). Toss Brussels sprouts with olive oil, salt, and pepper on a baking sheet. Spread in a single layer.
2. Roast for 20-25 minutes, until tender and edges are crispy, stirring halfway through.
3. While the Brussels sprouts are roasting, reduce the balsamic vinegar and honey in a small saucepan over medium heat until thickened, about 5 minutes.
4. Toss the roasted Brussels sprouts with the balsamic glaze and pecans, if using.
5. Serve warm, sprinkled with grated Parmesan cheese, if desired.

Nutritional Values:

- Calories: 140 per serving (without pecans and Parmesan)
- Protein: 4g
- Carbohydrates: 16g

- Fat: 7g
- Fiber: 4g

Garlic Parmesan Kale Chips

Ingredients:

- 1 large bunch of kale, stems removed and leaves torn into bite-sized pieces
- 2 tablespoons olive oil
- 2 cloves garlic, minced
- Salt and freshly ground black pepper, to taste
- 1/4 cup grated Parmesan cheese

Directions:

1. Preheat your oven to 300°F (150°C). Line a baking sheet with parchment paper.
2. In a large bowl, toss the kale pieces with olive oil, minced garlic, salt, and pepper until evenly coated.
3. Spread the kale in a single layer on the prepared baking sheet. Sprinkle with grated Parmesan cheese.
4. Bake for 10-15 minutes, or until the edges are crispy but not burnt.
5. Let cool slightly before serving. Enjoy these chips as a nutritious and flavorful snack.

Nutritional Values:

- Calories: 110 per serving (1/4 of the recipe)
- Protein: 5g
- Carbohydrates: 8g
- Fat: 7g
- Fiber: 2g

Quinoa Tabouli

Ingredients:

- 1 cup quinoa, cooked and cooled
- 1 cup fresh parsley, finely chopped
- 1/2 cup fresh mint, finely chopped
- 2 tomatoes, diced
- 1 cucumber, diced
- 1/4 cup red onion, finely chopped
- Juice of 2 lemons
- 2 tablespoons olive oil
- Salt and freshly ground black pepper, to taste

Directions:

1. In a large bowl, combine the cooked quinoa, parsley, mint, tomatoes, cucumber, and red onion.
2. In a small bowl, whisk together lemon juice, olive oil, salt, and pepper to create the dressing.
3. Pour the dressing over the quinoa mixture and toss until everything is well coated.
4. Chill in the refrigerator for at least 30 minutes before serving to allow the flavors to meld together.
5. Serve this refreshing quinoa tabouli as a side dish or a light snack.

Nutritional Values:

- Calories: 190 per serving (1/4 of the recipe)
- Protein: 6g
- Carbohydrates: 27g
- Fat: 7g
- Fiber: 4g

Spicy Edamame

Ingredients:

- 2 cups frozen edamame in pods
- 1 tablespoon olive oil
- 1 teaspoon sea salt
- 1/2 teaspoon chili flakes
- 1 teaspoon garlic powder
- Zest of 1 lemon

Directions:

1. Bring a pot of water to a boil and cook the edamame for 3-5 minutes, or until tender. Drain and pat dry.
2. In a bowl, toss the cooked edamame with olive oil, sea salt, chili flakes, garlic powder, and lemon zest until evenly coated.
3. Heat a skillet over medium-high heat. Add the edamame and sauté for 2-3 minutes, or until the pods are slightly charred.
4. Serve warm as a spicy and flavorful snack or side dish.

Nutritional Values:

- Calories: 150 per serving (1 cup)
- Protein: 12g
- Carbohydrates: 9g
- Fat: 8g
- Fiber: 4g

Stuffed Mini Bell Peppers

Ingredients:

- 12 mini bell peppers, halved and seeded
- 1 cup ricotta cheese
- 1/4 cup grated Parmesan cheese
- 1 tablespoon fresh basil, chopped
- 1 clove garlic, minced
- Salt and freshly ground black pepper, to taste
- 1/4 cup breadcrumbs
- 1 tablespoon olive oil

Directions:

1. Preheat your oven to 375°F (190°C). Arrange the bell pepper halves on a baking sheet.
2. In a bowl, mix together ricotta cheese, Parmesan cheese, basil, and garlic. Season with salt and pepper.
3. Fill each bell pepper half with the cheese mixture, then sprinkle with breadcrumbs.
4. Drizzle olive oil over the top of the stuffed peppers.
5. Bake for 20-25 minutes, or until the peppers are tender and the tops are golden brown.
6. Serve these stuffed mini bell peppers warm as a delicious and colorful snack or side.

Nutritional Values:

- Calories: 120 per serving (3 stuffed halves)
- Protein: 7g
- Carbohydrates: 8g
- Fat: 7g
- Fiber: 2g

Cucumber and Dill Greek Yogurt Dip

Ingredients:

- 2 cups Greek yogurt
- 1 cucumber, seeded and finely diced
- 2 tablespoons fresh dill, chopped
- 2 cloves garlic, minced
- 1 tablespoon lemon juice
- Salt and freshly ground black pepper, to taste

Directions:

1. In a medium bowl, combine the Greek yogurt, diced cucumber, fresh dill, minced garlic, and lemon juice. Mix well.
2. Season the dip with salt and pepper according to taste.
3. Refrigerate for at least 1 hour before serving to allow the flavors to meld together.
4. Serve the dip chilled with slices of fresh vegetables, pita chips, or as a refreshing condiment for grilled dishes.

Nutritional Values:

- Calories: 70 per serving (1/4 cup)
- Protein: 9g
- Carbohydrates: 5g
- Fat: 1g
- Fiber: 0.5g

Oven-Roasted Cauliflower Steaks

Ingredients:

- 1 large head cauliflower
- 2 tablespoons olive oil
- 1 teaspoon smoked paprika
- 1/2 teaspoon garlic powder
- Salt and freshly ground black pepper, to taste
- Fresh parsley, chopped, for garnish

Directions:

1. Preheat your oven to 400°F (200°C). Line a baking sheet with parchment paper.
2. Slice the cauliflower into 1/2-inch thick steaks, keeping the core intact to hold the slices together.
3. Brush each cauliflower steak on both sides with olive oil and season with smoked paprika, garlic powder, salt, and pepper.
4. Place the cauliflower steaks on the prepared baking sheet in a single layer.
5. Roast in the preheated oven for 25-30 minutes, or until tender and golden brown, flipping halfway through the cooking time.
6. Serve the cauliflower steaks garnished with chopped fresh parsley.

Nutritional Values:

- Calories: 120 per serving (1/4 of a large head)
- Protein: 4g
- Carbohydrates: 11g
- Fat: 7g
- Fiber: 5g

Parmesan Herb Popcorn

Ingredients:

- 1/2 cup popcorn kernels
- 2 tablespoons olive oil
- 1/4 cup grated Parmesan cheese
- 1 teaspoon dried oregano
- 1/2 teaspoon garlic powder
- Salt and freshly ground black pepper, to taste

Directions:

1. In a large pot, heat the olive oil over medium heat. Add the popcorn kernels and cover with a lid.
2. Shake the pot occasionally as the kernels pop. Once the popping slows to several seconds between pops, remove from heat.
3. In a small bowl, mix together the grated Parmesan cheese, dried oregano, garlic powder, salt, and pepper.
4. Pour the popped popcorn into a large bowl and while still warm, sprinkle the Parmesan herb mixture over it. Toss well to coat evenly.
5. Serve immediately for a savory, cheesy snack experience.

Nutritional Values:

- Calories: 150 per serving (1 cup popped)
- Protein: 4g
- Carbohydrates: 15g
- Fat: 8g
- Fiber: 3g

Beetroot and Goat Cheese Crostini

Ingredients:

- 1 baguette, sliced into 1/2-inch pieces
- 2 tablespoons olive oil
- 1 cup cooked beetroot, finely diced
- 1/2 cup goat cheese, softened
- 2 tablespoons balsamic reduction
- Fresh thyme leaves for garnish
- Salt and freshly ground black pepper, to taste

Directions:

1. Preheat your oven to 375°F (190°C). Brush both sides of the baguette slices with olive oil and place them on a baking sheet.
2. Toast the baguette slices in the oven for about 10 minutes, or until they are golden and crisp.
3. Spread a thin layer of goat cheese on each toasted baguette slice.
4. Top with a spoonful of diced beetroot, then drizzle with balsamic reduction.
5. Garnish each crostini with fresh thyme leaves and a sprinkle of salt and pepper.
6. Serve immediately as a colorful and flavorful appetizer or side dish.

Nutritional Values:

- Calories: 120 per serving (2 crostinis)
- Protein: 4g
- Carbohydrates: 14g
- Fat: 5g
- Fiber: 1g

Carrot Fries with Lemon Herb Dip

Ingredients for Carrot Fries:

- 4 large carrots, peeled and cut into sticks
- 2 tablespoons olive oil
- 1 teaspoon paprika
- Salt and freshly ground black pepper, to taste

Ingredients for Lemon Herb Dip:

- 1 cup Greek yogurt
- 1 tablespoon lemon juice
- 1 tablespoon fresh dill, chopped
- 1 tablespoon fresh parsley, chopped
- Salt and freshly ground black pepper, to taste

Directions:

1. Preheat the oven to 425°F (220°C). Line a baking sheet with parchment paper.
2. Toss the carrot sticks with olive oil, paprika, salt, and pepper. Arrange them in a single layer on the baking sheet.
3. Bake for 25-30 minutes, turning halfway through, until the carrots are tender and slightly crispy.
4. While the carrots are baking, prepare the dip by mixing together Greek yogurt, lemon juice, dill, parsley, salt, and pepper in a small bowl.
5. Serve the carrot fries hot with the lemon herb dip on the side.

Nutritional Values:

- Calories: 180 per serving (1/4 of the recipe)
- Protein: 5g
- Carbohydrates: 24g
- Fat: 8g

- Fiber: 5g

Mushroom and Garlic Bruschetta

Ingredients:

- 1 baguette, sliced into 1/2-inch thick slices
- 1/4 cup olive oil, divided
- 2 cups mushrooms, finely chopped (a mix of shiitake, cremini, and button)
- 3 cloves garlic, minced
- 2 tablespoons fresh parsley, chopped
- Salt and freshly ground black pepper, to taste
- 1/4 cup grated Parmesan cheese (optional)

Directions:

1. Preheat your oven to 375°F (190°C). Brush the baguette slices with half of the olive oil and place them on a baking sheet. Toast in the oven for 8-10 minutes, or until golden.
2. Heat the remaining olive oil in a skillet over medium heat. Add the mushrooms and garlic, sautéing until the mushrooms are tender and all the moisture has evaporated.
3. Stir in the parsley, and season with salt and pepper.
4. Top each toasted baguette slice with the mushroom mixture. Sprinkle with Parmesan cheese if using.
5. Broil for 2-3 minutes, or until the cheese is melted and slightly golden.
6. Serve immediately, offering a savory and elegant appetizer or side.

Nutritional Values:

- Calories: 220 per serving (3 slices)
- Protein: 7g
- Carbohydrates: 27g

- Fat: 10g
- Fiber: 2g

Cheesy Spinach Pinwheels

Ingredients:

- 1 puff pastry sheet, thawed
- 1 cup fresh spinach, finely chopped
- 1/2 cup ricotta cheese
- 1/4 cup feta cheese, crumbled
- 1 garlic clove, minced
- Salt and freshly ground black pepper, to taste
- 1 egg, beaten (for egg wash)

Directions:

1. Preheat your oven to 400°F (200°C). Line a baking sheet with parchment paper.
2. In a bowl, combine the spinach, ricotta cheese, feta cheese, garlic, salt, and pepper.
3. Roll out the puff pastry on a lightly floured surface. Spread the spinach and cheese mixture evenly over the pastry, leaving a small border around the edges.
4. Roll the pastry up tightly, then cut into 1-inch thick slices.
5. Place the slices, cut side down, on the prepared baking sheet. Brush the tops with the beaten egg.
6. Bake for 15-20 minutes, or until golden brown and puffed up.
7. Serve warm, ideal for a comforting snack or a savory side dish.

Nutritional Values:

- Calories: 180 per serving (1 pinwheel)
- Protein: 5g
- Carbohydrates: 12g

- Fat: 12g
- Fiber: 1g

Sweet and Spicy Roasted Chickpeas

Ingredients:

- 1 can (15 oz) chickpeas, drained, rinsed, and dried
- 1 tablespoon olive oil
- 1 tablespoon honey (or maple syrup for a vegan option)
- 1/2 teaspoon smoked paprika
- 1/2 teaspoon ground cumin
- 1/4 teaspoon cayenne pepper (adjust to taste)
- Salt, to taste

Directions:

1. Preheat your oven to 375°F (190°C). Line a baking sheet with parchment paper.
2. In a bowl, toss the chickpeas with olive oil, honey, smoked paprika, cumin, cayenne pepper, and salt until evenly coated.
3. Spread the chickpeas in a single layer on the prepared baking sheet.
4. Roast for 25-30 minutes, stirring occasionally, until crispy and golden.
5. Let cool slightly before serving. Enjoy as a crunchy, sweet, and spicy snack or as a flavorful addition to salads and soups.

Nutritional Values:

- Calories: 160 per serving (1/4 of the recipe)
- Protein: 6g
- Carbohydrates: 22g
- Fat: 5g
- Fiber: 6g

Broccoli and Cheddar Stuffed Potato Skins

Ingredients:

- 4 large russet potatoes
- 2 tablespoons olive oil
- Salt and freshly ground black pepper, to taste
- 1 cup broccoli florets, finely chopped
- 1 cup sharp cheddar cheese, shredded
- 1/4 cup sour cream
- 2 green onions, thinly sliced
- 1/4 teaspoon paprika

Directions:

1. Preheat your oven to 400°F (200°C). Pierce the potatoes with a fork and bake for 50-60 minutes, or until tender. Let cool slightly.
2. Cut the potatoes in half lengthwise and scoop out the flesh, leaving a thin layer attached to the skin. Reserve the scooped potato for another use.
3. Brush the potato skins inside and out with olive oil and season with salt and pepper. Place skin-side up on a baking sheet and bake for 10 minutes.
4. Flip the skins, fill each with broccoli and top with cheddar cheese. Sprinkle with paprika. Bake for another 10-15 minutes, until the cheese is melted and bubbly.
5. Serve the potato skins warm, topped with a dollop of sour cream and sprinkled with green onions.

Nutritional Values:

- Calories: 220 per serving (2 halves)
- Protein: 8g
- Carbohydrates: 18g

- Fat: 13g
- Fiber: 2g

Tomato Basil Mozzarella Salad

Ingredients:

- 2 cups cherry tomatoes, halved
- 8 oz fresh mozzarella cheese, cubed
- 1/4 cup fresh basil leaves, torn
- 2 tablespoons extra virgin olive oil
- 1 tablespoon balsamic vinegar
- Salt and freshly ground black pepper, to taste

Directions:

1. In a large bowl, combine the cherry tomatoes, mozzarella cheese, and basil leaves.
2. Drizzle with olive oil and balsamic vinegar. Gently toss to combine.
3. Season with salt and pepper to taste.
4. Let the salad sit for 10 minutes before serving to allow the flavors to meld together.
5. Serve as a refreshing and flavorful side dish or snack.

Nutritional Values:

- Calories: 180 per serving (1/4 of the recipe)
- Protein: 9g
- Carbohydrates: 6g
- Fat: 14g
- Fiber: 1g

Grilled Eggplant Rolls with Herbed Ricotta

Ingredients:

- 2 medium eggplants, sliced lengthwise into 1/4-inch thick strips
- 2 tablespoons olive oil
- Salt and freshly ground black pepper, to taste
- 1 cup ricotta cheese
- 2 tablespoons fresh basil, chopped
- 1 tablespoon fresh parsley, chopped
- 1 clove garlic, minced
- 1/4 cup grated Parmesan cheese
- 1/2 cup baby spinach leaves

Directions:

1. Preheat your grill to medium-high heat. Brush both sides of the eggplant slices with olive oil and season with salt and pepper.
2. Grill the eggplant slices for 2-3 minutes on each side, until tender and grill marks appear. Remove from the grill and let cool slightly.
3. In a bowl, mix together the ricotta cheese, basil, parsley, garlic, and Parmesan cheese. Season with salt and pepper to taste.
4. Place a spoonful of the ricotta mixture at one end of each eggplant slice, top with a few spinach leaves, and roll up tightly.
5. Serve the eggplant rolls immediately, or chill in the refrigerator before serving as a cold snack or side dish.

Nutritional Values:

- Calories: 120 per serving (2 rolls)
- Protein: 5g
- Carbohydrates: 8g
- Fat: 8g
- Fiber: 3g

Savory Pumpkin Seed and Rosemary Crackers

Ingredients:

- 1 cup whole wheat flour
- 1/2 cup pumpkin seeds, finely ground
- 2 tablespoons fresh rosemary, finely chopped
- 1/2 teaspoon salt
- 1/4 teaspoon black pepper
- 1/4 cup water
- 2 tablespoons olive oil

Directions:

1. Preheat your oven to 350°F (175°C). Line a baking sheet with parchment paper.
2. In a bowl, combine the whole wheat flour, ground pumpkin seeds, rosemary, salt, and pepper.
3. Stir in the water and olive oil until a dough forms. Knead briefly until smooth.
4. Roll out the dough on a lightly floured surface to 1/8-inch thickness. Cut into desired shapes using a cookie cutter or knife.
5. Place the crackers on the prepared baking sheet. Prick each cracker with a fork to prevent puffing.
6. Bake for 15-20 minutes, or until the crackers are crisp and golden brown. Let cool on a wire rack.
7. Serve the crackers as a snack on their own or with dips and spreads.

Nutritional Values:

- Calories: 90 per serving (3 crackers)
- Protein: 3g
- Carbohydrates: 9g

- Fat: 5g
- Fiber: 2g

A 4-Week Meal Plan

Week 1 Vegetarian Meal Plan

Welcome to the first week of your vegetarian journey! Below, you'll find a comprehensive meal plan that excludes the specific recipes you've requested to be left out. Each day is organized with breakfast, lunch, dinner, and two snack options, ensuring a balanced and varied diet throughout the week. Also included are weekly shopping lists to simplify your grocery runs and tips for customizing the meal plan to fit your individual dietary needs and preferences.

Day 1

- **Breakfast:** Zesty Lemon-Ricotta Pancakes
- **Lunch:** Beetroot and Feta Cheese Salad
- **Dinner:** Lemon Garlic Pasta with Broccoli
- **Snacks:** Cheesy Spinach Pinwheels, Sweet and Spicy Roasted Chickpeas

Day 2

- **Breakfast:** Savory Spinach and Cheese Breakfast Muffins
- **Lunch:** Warm Spinach and Artichoke Tart
- **Dinner:** Eggplant Parmesan Tower
- **Snacks:** Broccoli and Cheddar Stuffed Potato Skins, Tomato Basil Mozzarella Salad

Day 3

- **Breakfast:** Golden Turmeric and Ginger Oatmeal
- **Lunch:** Lemon Herb Couscous Salad
- **Dinner:** Garden Vegetable Lasagna
- **Snacks:** Sweet Potato Hummus, Parmesan Herb Popcorn

Day 4

- **Breakfast:** Savory Breakfast Sweet Potato Bowls
- **Lunch:** Classic Tomato Basil Soup
- **Dinner:** Cauliflower Steak with Chimichurri Sauce
- **Snacks:** Stuffed Mini Bell Peppers, Quinoa Tabouli

Day 5

- **Breakfast:** Toasted Coconut and Chia Seed Parfait
- **Lunch:** Mediterranean Stuffed Bell Peppers
- **Dinner:** Zesty Thai Green Curry with Vegetables
- **Snacks:** Crispy Baked Zucchini Fries, Garlic Parmesan Kale Chips

Day 6

- **Breakfast:** Almond Butter and Banana Stuffed French Toast
- **Lunch:** Spicy Black Bean Soup
- **Dinner:** Butternut Squash and Sage Gnocchi
- **Snacks:** Roasted Brussels Sprouts with Balsamic Glaze, Oven-Roasted Cauliflower Steaks

Day 7

- **Breakfast:** Pear and Walnut Baked Oatmeal
- **Lunch:** Asian-Inspired Tofu Noodle Bowl
- **Dinner:** Walnut and Lentil Bolognese
- **Snacks:** Cucumber and Dill Greek Yogurt Dip, Beetroot and Goat Cheese Crostini

Weekly Shopping List

To make your preparation as easy as possible, compile a shopping list based on the recipes chosen for the week. Remember to adjust quantities based on your serving needs.

- **Fruits and Vegetables:** Lemons, beetroots, feta cheese, broccoli, spinach, artichokes, eggplant, garlic, ginger, sweet potatoes, coconuts, bell peppers, zucchini, Brussels sprouts, cauliflower, pears, walnuts, cucumbers, dill, tomatoes, avocados, onions, mushrooms, butternut squash, kale, carrots, chickpeas, potatoes
- **Grains and Bakery:** Quinoa, couscous, pasta, bread (for bruschetta and panini), oatmeal, popcorn, tortillas for quesadillas
- **Dairy and Eggs:** Ricotta cheese, cheddar cheese, mozzarella cheese, goat cheese, eggs, yogurt, milk (or plant-based alternatives)
- **Pantry Staples:** Olive oil, vinegar (balsamic, red wine), sun-dried tomatoes, black beans, lentils, chickpeas, spices (turmeric, ginger, basil, rosemary, salt, pepper), honey, almond butter, coconut flakes, chia seeds, walnuts, canned tomatoes, vegetable broth, curry paste, truffle oil, pesto, pine nuts, nutritional yeast
- **Proteins:** Tofu
- **Miscellaneous:** Nuts (almonds, walnuts), seeds (pumpkin, sunflower), crackers, baking ingredients (flour, baking powder, etc.)

Adjusting the Plan

- **Allergies and Intolerances:** Substitute nuts, dairy, and gluten-containing ingredients with suitable alternatives. For instance, use almond milk instead of cow's milk, gluten-free bread, or chickpea flour instead of traditional flour.
- **Portion Sizes:** Adjust portion sizes according to dietary needs and goals. If aiming for weight loss, focus on increasing vegetables and reducing high-calorie ingredients. For weight gain or higher energy needs, add more protein-rich foods like tofu and nuts, and consider larger portions.
- **Preference Adjustments:** Feel free to swap out ingredients based on personal taste preferences or seasonal availability. The recipes provided are flexible and can accommodate a variety of substitutions.

Week 2 Vegetarian Meal Plan

Embark on the second week of your vegetarian adventure with a fresh set of meals designed to provide variety and nutrition. Similar to week 1, each day offers a breakfast, lunch, dinner, and two snacks. We continue to ensure that your meals are diverse, satisfying, and align with a vegetarian lifestyle. Additionally, a new shopping list for this week will assist in making your grocery shopping hassle-free.

Day 8

- **Breakfast:** Avocado and Egg Breakfast Pizza
- **Lunch:** Roasted Vegetable and Quinoa Wrap
- **Dinner:** Stuffed Portobello Mushrooms with Spinach and Goat Cheese
- **Snacks:** Avocado and Chickpea Salad, Mushroom and Garlic Bruschetta

Day 9

- **Breakfast:** Cinnamon Quinoa Breakfast Bowl
- **Lunch:** Curried Lentil and Sweet Potato Bowls
- **Dinner:** Quinoa Stuffed Bell Peppers
- **Snacks:** Crispy Baked Zucchini Fries, Sweet Potato Hummus

Day 10

- **Breakfast:** Pear and Walnut Baked Oatmeal
- **Lunch:** Grilled Portobello Mushroom Burgers
- **Dinner:** Eggplant Parmesan Tower
- **Snacks:** Quinoa Tabouli, Garlic Parmesan Kale Chips

Day 11

- **Breakfast:** Zesty Lemon-Ricotta Pancakes
- **Lunch:** Avocado, Tomato, and Mozzarella Panini
- **Dinner:** Garden Vegetable Lasagna

- **Snacks:** Oven-Roasted Cauliflower Steaks, Tomato Basil Mozzarella Salad

Day 12

- **Breakfast:** Savory Breakfast Sweet Potato Bowls
- **Lunch:** Mediterranean Chickpea Salad
- **Dinner:** Cauliflower Steak with Chimichurri Sauce
- **Snacks:** Stuffed Mini Bell Peppers, Sweet and Spicy Roasted Chickpeas

Day 13

- **Breakfast:** Golden Turmeric and Ginger Oatmeal
- **Lunch:** Zucchini Ribbon and Cherry Tomato Pasta Salad
- **Dinner:** Roasted Butternut Squash Risotto
- **Snacks:** Beetroot and Goat Cheese Crostini, Cucumber and Dill Greek Yogurt Dip

Day 14

- **Breakfast:** Toasted Coconut and Chia Seed Parfait
- **Lunch:** Eggplant and Chickpea Stew
- **Dinner:** Wild Mushroom and Truffle Oil Risotto
- **Snacks:** Cheesy Spinach Pinwheels, Parmesan Herb Popcorn

Weekly Shopping List Week 2

- **Fruits and Vegetables:** Avocados, eggs, quinoa, spinach, portobello mushrooms, sweet potatoes, lentils, bell peppers, zucchini, tomatoes, mozzarella cheese, cauliflower, chickpeas, butternut squash, garlic, ginger, lemons, onions, eggplant, various lettuce for salads, cherry tomatoes, fresh herbs (basil, cilantro, parsley)
- **Grains and Bakery:** Breakfast cereal (for the quinoa bowl), bread (for panini and bruschetta), lasagna noodles, risotto rice, pasta

- **Dairy and Eggs:** Ricotta cheese, goat cheese, parmesan cheese, eggs, mozzarella cheese, milk (or plant-based alternatives for vegan options)
- **Pantry Staples:** Olive oil, balsamic vinegar, quinoa, lentils, canned tomatoes, vegetable broth, curry powder, truffle oil, pine nuts, sun-dried tomatoes, chickpeas, nuts (for snacks and garnishing), seeds (pumpkin, sunflower), crackers, popcorn
- **Proteins:** Tofu (as a meat substitute in some recipes)
- **Miscellaneous:** Nutritional yeast (for a cheesy flavor in vegan dishes), tahini (for hummus), spices (turmeric, ginger, basil, rosemary, salt, pepper, chili flakes)

Adjusting the Plan for Week 2

- **Flexibility:** This plan remains adaptable. Feel free to interchange lunch and dinner options based on your schedule and preferences.
- **Dietary Adjustments:** For gluten sensitivities, ensure that all grains and bakery items are gluten-free. For lactose intolerance, choose lactose-free dairy or plant-based alternatives.
- **Flavor Preferences:** Customize spices and herbs according to taste. If you prefer milder flavors, reduce the quantity of spices like chili flakes and ginger.

Week 3 Vegetarian Meal Plan

Welcome to week 3 of your vegetarian meal plan, designed to infuse your diet with a wide array of flavors and nutrients. This week continues to offer a structured plan with breakfast, lunch, dinner, and snack options, all selected to provide a balanced and exciting culinary experience. Here's your detailed plan along with a new shopping list for ease and convenience.

Day 15

- **Breakfast:** Creamy Mushroom and Spinach Omelette
- **Lunch:** Grilled Vegetable and Goat Cheese Sandwich
- **Dinner:** Lemon Garlic Pasta with Broccoli
- **Snacks:** Savory Pumpkin Seed and Rosemary Crackers, Oven-Roasted Cauliflower Steaks

Day 16

- **Breakfast:** Mixed Berry and Almond Smoothie
- **Lunch:** Pesto Pasta with Sun-Dried Tomatoes and Pine Nuts
- **Dinner:** Quinoa Stuffed Bell Peppers
- **Snacks:** Sweet and Spicy Roasted Chickpeas, Cucumber and Dill Greek Yogurt Dip

Day 17

- **Breakfast:** Avocado Toast with Heirloom Tomatoes
- **Lunch:** Classic Tomato Basil Soup
- **Dinner:** Butternut Squash and Sage Gnocchi
- **Snacks:** Tomato Basil Mozzarella Salad, Cheesy Spinach Pinwheels

Day 18

- **Breakfast:** Blueberry Lemon Breakfast Bars
- **Lunch:** Spicy Black Bean Soup
- **Dinner:** Garden Vegetable Lasagna

- **Snacks:** Beetroot and Goat Cheese Crostini, Garlic Parmesan Kale Chips

Day 19

- **Breakfast:** Pear and Walnut Baked Oatmeal
- **Lunch:** Curried Lentil and Sweet Potato Bowls
- **Dinner:** Walnut and Lentil Bolognese
- **Snacks:** Quinoa Tabouli, Sweet Potato Hummus

Day 20

- **Breakfast:** Zesty Lemon-Ricotta Pancakes
- **Lunch:** Lemon Herb Couscous Salad
- **Dinner:** Eggplant Parmesan Tower
- **Snacks:** Stuffed Mini Bell Peppers, Roasted Brussels Sprouts with Balsamic Glaze

Day 21

- **Breakfast:** Savory Breakfast Sweet Potato Bowls
- **Lunch:** Avocado, Tomato, and Mozzarella Panini
- **Dinner:** Zesty Thai Green Curry with Vegetables
- **Snacks:** Crispy Baked Zucchini Fries, Mushroom and Garlic Bruschetta

Weekly Shopping List Week 3

- **Fruits and Vegetables:** Broccoli, spinach, mushrooms, mixed berries, almonds, avocados, heirloom tomatoes, lemons, butternut squash, sage, blueberries, sweet potatoes, lentils, walnuts, bell peppers, garlic, cucumbers, dill, kale, Brussels sprouts
- **Grains and Bakery:** Oatmeal, pasta, quinoa, bread for panini and toast, breakfast bars (or ingredients to make your own), couscous
- **Dairy and Eggs:** Eggs, goat cheese, mozzarella cheese, ricotta cheese, parmesan cheese, milk (or plant-based alternatives)

- **Pantry Staples:** Olive oil, sun-dried tomatoes, pine nuts, canned tomatoes, vegetable broth, curry paste, spices (turmeric, ginger, basil, rosemary, salt, pepper), nuts (for snacks), seeds (pumpkin, sunflower), crackers, popcorn
- **Proteins:** Black beans, chickpeas, lentils, tofu (optional for additional protein in salads or bowls)
- **Miscellaneous:** Nutritional yeast, tahini, vinegar (balsamic, red wine)

Adjusting the Plan for Week 3

- **Customization:** As before, adjust recipes based on your dietary needs and flavor preferences. Swap out any ingredients for their seasonal counterparts or whatever you have on hand.
- **Protein Variations:** Consider incorporating plant-based protein powders into smoothies or breakfast bars for an extra protein boost.
- **Meal Prepping:** Many of these meals can be prepped in advance. Consider making larger batches of quinoa, roasted vegetables, or soups and storing them for quick assembly during busy days.

Week 4 Vegetarian Meal Plan

As you enter the fourth week of your vegetarian meal journey, the focus remains on variety, nutrition, and ease of preparation. This week's meal plan introduces a new set of delicious recipes to keep your meals exciting and satisfying. Here's your day-by-day guide, along with a comprehensive shopping list for the week.

Day 22

- **Breakfast:** Spinach and Goat Cheese Breakfast Quesadillas
- **Lunch:** Quinoa, Black Bean, and Corn Salad
- **Dinner:** Roasted Red Pepper Pasta
- **Snacks:** Savory Pumpkin Seed and Rosemary Crackers, Carrot Fries with Lemon Herb Dip

Day 23

- **Breakfast:** Golden Turmeric and Ginger Oatmeal
- **Lunch:** Mediterranean Chickpea Salad
- **Dinner:** Smoky Red Pepper and Chickpea Soup
- **Snacks:** Beetroot and Goat Cheese Crostini, Sweet and Spicy Roasted Chickpeas

Day 24

- **Breakfast:** Cinnamon Quinoa Breakfast Bowl
- **Lunch:** Caprese Stuffed Avocado
- **Dinner:** Chickpea and Spinach Stuffed Portobello Mushrooms
- **Snacks:** Crispy Baked Zucchini Fries, Parmesan Herb Popcorn

Day 25

- **Breakfast:** Zesty Lemon-Ricotta Pancakes
- **Lunch:** Lemon Herb Couscous Salad
- **Dinner:** Eggplant Parmesan Tower
- **Snacks:** Stuffed Mini Bell Peppers, Garlic Parmesan Kale Chips

Day 26

- **Breakfast:** Toasted Coconut and Chia Seed Parfait
- **Lunch:** Sweet Potato and Kale Hash
- **Dinner:** Grilled Vegetable and Goat Cheese Panzanella
- **Snacks:** Oven-Roasted Cauliflower Steaks, Tomato Basil Mozzarella Salad

Day 27

- **Breakfast:** Almond Butter and Banana Stuffed French Toast
- **Lunch:** Zucchini Ribbon and Cherry Tomato Pasta Salad
- **Dinner:** Walnut and Lentil Bolognese
- **Snacks:** Quinoa Tabouli, Sweet Potato Hummus

Day 28

- **Breakfast:** Avocado and Egg Breakfast Pizza
- **Lunch:** Asian-Inspired Tofu Noodle Bowl
- **Dinner:** Zesty Thai Green Curry with Vegetables
- **Snacks:** Cucumber and Dill Greek Yogurt Dip, Mushroom and Garlic Bruschetta

Weekly Shopping List Week 4

- **Fruits and Vegetables:** Spinach, goat cheese, quinoa, black beans, corn, red peppers, carrots, ginger, avocados, tomatoes, chickpeas, zucchini, kale, cauliflower, lemons, bananas, sweet potatoes
- **Grains and Bakery:** Bread for quesadillas, pasta, couscous, breakfast cereal for the quinoa bowl, noodles for the tofu bowl
- **Dairy and Eggs:** Eggs, ricotta cheese, mozzarella cheese, goat cheese, parmesan cheese, milk (or plant-based alternatives)
- **Pantry Staples:** Olive oil, sun-dried tomatoes, pine nuts, vegetable broth, spices (turmeric, ginger, basil, rosemary, salt, pepper), nuts (almonds), seeds (chia, pumpkin, sunflower), popcorn, canned tomatoes, curry paste
- **Proteins:** Tofu, lentils, chickpeas

- **Miscellaneous:** Nutritional yeast for a cheesy flavor, tahini for dips, balsamic vinegar, lemon herb dip ingredients

Adjusting the Plan for Week 4

- **Customization Options:** Feel free to swap out ingredients based on availability or personal preference. For example, if you're not a fan of goat cheese, try substituting it with feta or a dairy-free alternative.
- **Meal Prepping Tips:** Many of these dishes can be prepared in advance. Consider spending some time at the beginning of the week cooking grains like quinoa and pasta, roasting vegetables, and preparing breakfast items like the oatmeal and parfait components.
- **Dealing with Leftovers:** Incorporate any leftovers into creative new dishes. For example, leftover roasted vegetables can be added to salads, quesadillas, or wraps to enhance their flavor and nutritional value.

This week's plan aims to keep your meals diverse and your palate intrigued, rounding out a full month of vegetarian eating with health and flavor at the forefront. Enjoy the culinary adventure!

Conclusion: Embracing Vegetarianism

As we close this chapter on vegetarianism, it's important to remember that embarking on a journey toward a more plant-based lifestyle is both a personal and transformative experience. Like any great adventure, it's filled with discoveries, challenges, and joys. Whether you're taking your first steps into vegetarianism or you're looking to deepen your commitment, know that every meal is an opportunity to nourish not only your body but also the planet.

The Journey Ahead

Embarking on a vegetarian journey is a deeply personal choice that unfolds uniquely for everyone. It's a path paved with intention, curiosity, and discovery. Take it at your own pace. There's beauty in every step, whether you're exploring meatless Mondays, diving into vegetarianism, or transitioning to a fully plant-based diet. Remember, it's not about perfection; it's about making choices that align with your values and well-being.

Community and Support

No journey should be taken alone, and thankfully, the vegetarian community is vibrant, welcoming, and ever-growing. From local vegetarian groups and online forums to plant-based cooking classes and social media platforms, there are numerous resources available to support you. These communities can offer advice, share recipes, and provide encouragement. Connecting with others who share your dietary lifestyle can turn challenges into shared experiences and victories. Don't hesitate to reach out, ask questions, and engage. The support you'll find is invaluable.

Continual Learning

The world of vegetarian cooking is rich and boundless. There's always a new ingredient to discover, a technique to master, or a cuisine to explore. Let your curiosity lead the way. Embrace the process of learning and experimentation. Cooking is a creative endeavor that allows for endless exploration and expression. Visit local farmers' markets, subscribe to vegetarian cooking blogs, watch tutorials from chefs, and don't be afraid to experiment in your own kitchen. Each recipe you try and every meal you create is a step forward in your journey.

Remember, embracing vegetarianism is more than just a dietary change; it's a lifestyle that celebrates and respects life, health, and the environment. It's a choice that contributes to a more sustainable and compassionate world. So here's to the journey ahead — may it be filled with discovery, joy, and, of course, delicious vegetarian fare. Let the adventure begin!

www.ingramcontent.com/pod-product-compliance
Lightning Source LLC
Chambersburg PA
CBHW072211070526
44585CB00015B/1294